Why Not A Woman President

Why not a Woman President

Lolu Adebayo

Published by Lolu Adebayo, 2024.

While every precaution has been taken in the preparation of this book, the publisher assumes no responsibility for errors or omissions, or for damages resulting from the use of the information contained herein.

WHY NOT A WOMAN PRESIDENT

First edition. September 27, 2024.

ISBN: 979-8227479488

Written by Lolu Adebayo.

Also by Lolu Adebayo

Why not a Woman President

Table of Contents

This book is dedicated to

*My parents: Madam Ayodele Bernice Adebayo, R.I.P. &
Chief Elijah Ogidiolu Adebayo, R.I.P.*

My sisters: Clara, Veronica, Catherine, Folashade

My brothers: Tim, Ola, Ade (R.I.P.), Tope, Taiye

To Aisha Adebayo for her extraordinary

contribution and support and to everybody on earth.

Let's promote love and peace so we can all live in

harmony.

And finally, to all the women in the world, we love

you!

Why Not A Woman President

It's About Time ...
Lolu Adebayo B.Sc., M.IT

Contents

7

Preface

his is like an order of nature for us, from the beginning of time as
far back as Adam and Eve. As we all know, men have been in charge
or supposed to be in charge. We could all realize things are not really
getting better mainly because men are generally egotistic, chauvinistic,
and exhibit superiority complexes; unfortunately, things are not
getting better as per world order and progress. We tend to see women as
second-class, but come to think of it, back to the law of nature, majority
of women are always doing a better job in nurturing their family—one
of the many reasons most women should be in a better position to be
leaders.
As men, we always argue that majority of us provide the financial
aid for our families, but if that's the case, since most of us men lack the
ability to nurture our family to be useful to the society, then we could
offer to finance the women to *nurture* the world with their motherly
qualities now as our president. We are boxed in the ideology of
being the gender to reckon with all the time, and the female should wait
till eternity.
The purpose of this book is to create *awareness* among all people

about the legitimacy of women's skills and natural attributes that qualify

them to be *equal,* if not better, for the democratic appointment as a

president and commander in chief especially in the developed countries.

The computer era has improved our ability to communicate efficiently

globally. The world in this millennium is like a big village, so it's about

time to take advantage of this unique means of communication and

spread the awareness worldwide, with the availability of the Internet, or

the worldwide web. We can now email, blog and chat online promoting

"EQUAL RIGHTS AND JUSTICE FOR ALL PEOPLE"

T

8

the awareness and leave behind the old ways of our beliefs as per women's
limited role, incompetence, and less capable in politics—then promote
this *overdue* issue of women presidency.

"Because man and woman are the compliment of one another, we need woman's thought in national affairs to make a safe and stable government."
—Elizabeth Cady Stanton (1815-1902)
"EQUAL RIGHTS AND JUSTICE FOR ALL PEOPLE"

9

Political theories, Ideologies, and no Action

M

ost of our political leaders all over the world have their own or their
party ideologies and agendas to make life better for the *common
people* (the masses), but once elected, most of their promises could
not be accomplished. Either they were not practicable or had hindrances
and opposition from the other party; eventually nothing gets done, and
the common people end up suffering. A lot of agendas were promised, and
not acting on them had been a hindrance to the progress in most countries
especially in the third World countries.
Most of these the third world countries got their independence for so
many years with no progress in sight, and the situation is getting worse.
These countries have the natural and human resources but always
terrible management probably due to bad leadership, but hopefully these
countries will wake up soon from this *nightmare.* The undeveloped
countries remained undeveloped and are deteriorating. And
the First World countries, (Developed countries) because of the same

unimplemented ideologies and agendas promised to the masses during

election campaigns, make things more difficult for the common people.

I don't like the classification "Third World countries."

Which countries are Second World countries? Hopefully the Third World

countries can get good government first; then they could dream about

women presidents. Although, Liberia once elected a woman president. But

notwithstanding, most Third World countries are still growing toward a

"EQUAL RIGHTS AND JUSTICE FOR ALL PEOPLE"

10

legitimate and reliable democratic system. Then they might be invited to

the "Super 50" summit.

One of the many reasons I was delighted to see a black man winning

a presidential election in one of the Developed World countries; and hopefully

the elected presidents in the Third World countries could finally follow

his good deeds and influence their thinking and that they are not in

government for themselves and their immediate families, friends, and

concubines but for the people—most especially the common people.

To be realistic, the Third World countries are not ready for a woman

president: not that it is bad thing, but the level of male chauvinism is

so ridiculous with the barbaric beliefs that "the woman's place is in the

kitchen." In some of these countries, women cannot even get a driver's

license unless accompanied by a man.

Most underdeveloped countries do not even believe in women's

education, which is the key to most achievements and a good prerequisite

to leadership, but hopefully it will happen soon, because the

so-called Developed World countries one-time deprived women from casting political votes for ages. As men we have been ruling the world from the

beginning of time, and we could now see the extent of the *ignorance* and

disconnection to reality. Any task you have tried so hard to achieve

and always failed, then it is better to give the other group the chance to

take a shot at it; and hopefully the women will prevail and make this

world of ours better.

We should all compliment China and India (both these

countries are still grouped as "Developing countries" or Third World Countries)

for their efforts. Billions of dollars were invested into the *millennium growth*

projects by the "Developed countries" for development, and it was only

China and India that showed signs of growth/development because of their

individual economic advancement, and we should all watch out! China

was reported recently to be on her way up to be the financial leader of

the world soon; hope most of the other developing countries

could emulate these countries like China, especially in the continent of Africa.

Most countries in Africa have the human power and natural resources

as China and India, or better, but the problem in Africa is leadership.

and now all eyes are on Africa—the world is watching. But I

have the intuition that with the new generation and leadership,
Africa will rise to the occasion and finally become a continent to reckon
with and not pity.
"EQUAL RIGHTS AND JUSTICE FOR ALL PEOPLE"

11

I am not playing the devil's advocate, but I think most leaders in
the developing countries could be good leaders but corrupted by
the

international negative influences because most of the aid from
the

developed countries or the International Monetary Fund (IMF),
either

financial or other form of aid, were approved based on various
conditions

and many times, not good for the common people (the masses),
especially

when some of the so-called leaders got greedy and failed to
implement

the main purpose of the aid.

Politics could be entertaining especially during election time,
and

we all enjoy the negative advertisements (Jokes) by our
politicians

during the rat race, but now, the common people are really

suffering, and we are not really finding those outrageous
advertisements

funny compared to when things were good for us financially. So,
we

suggest our political leaders worldwide should be more
compassionate

and focus more on how to make things better for the common
people

through bipartisan efforts whenever necessary. Once things get
better

again, hopefully soon, we will continue to enjoy

your jokes. We are not asking for handouts but to create jobs for us to

have a life and improve the economy as good citizens.

"You are the people who are shaping a better world. One of the secrets of

inner peace is the practice of compassion."

—Dalai Lama (1935-)

You define your ideology as what makes you to be identified or

grouped as a conservative, liberal, or moderate; but I identified my

ideology as still "sitting on the wall." To emphasize my stands on this

kind of grouping, in the 2008 election in the United States, I wished

Hillary Clinton won all the way because I wanted a woman to show me

what they can do; and to me, she was the one representing that gender.

I believed she would be able to manage or the ability to preside

better—being a president or a manager is having good people around

you to do the work you have been appointed for. And because of the

nurturing ability and patience of women, I thought she could have better

intuition to resolve matters with the help of her qualified aides and

advisers.

My family were all for President Obama, and he was definitely my

second choice not because I was all the way for the Democrats; but

"EQUAL RIGHTS AND JUSTICE FOR ALL PEOPLE"

12

because he is intelligent, eloquent, fit, and to be honest, black. Either

way, I just wanted history to happen. All my family perceived me like an

outcast for picking Clinton; they think that because I like Bill Clinton, it

was the main reason why I wanted the wife to win.

But that was not the reason, although I liked Bill Clinton, and again

not because he is a Democrat. It's just a natural liking (he is likable

person), he was just like a celebrity, and another thing I supported

him to win the second term was because he did a good job during his

first term: but some people argued he was just *at the right place*

at the right time. What was wrong with that? We all wish to be at the

right place at the right time, but we still must do some things right to

maintain that good fortune.

I like President Obama too, and don't get me wrong because my

preferred candidate lost. He was my second choice, again not

because he was a Democrat but because he is intelligent and belongs to

the black race. I thought he did not have a good chance because of his

race and my race too, but I was wrong.

My thinking was that it would be a miracle to see a black American president so soon, and I was avoiding a big disappointment supporting

him all the way; and since the Clintons were household names, things

might go their way. So, I had a better chance to fulfill my dream and see

a *woman president,* but I was surprised that most women were reluctant

to support her and that was basically from the brainwash of women by

men from the beginning of time, that women are not competent for that

level of responsibility as a president. President Obama did a very good

job, and he salvaged the United States of America (USA)

from the financial downturn which was global, and his input in world peace.

Most of the time we expect too much from the presidents, as if

they are superhuman or saints. Again, as a manager (president in this

situation), if some of the assistants are not really pulling their weight,

you as president still get the blame for the poor performance of the

administration. *But* I do still wish to see a woman in that presidential

position especially in the United States and most developed countries.

As I mention later in this book, we should all support and encourage

our government to continue spending money on projects to create more jobs. Then the masses will be comfortable to spend more to improve the

"EQUAL RIGHTS AND JUSTICE FOR ALL PEOPLE"

13

economy, and later we could act on reducing or eliminating the deficit. I

know some groups of people would prefer the *deficit reduction* to be the

priority now. Government spending more and getting involved

in so many projects are truly creating more and "bigger" government. But

now, the government must get more involved because we

are all in a tough situation financially, which needs more participation

from our governments; and the deficit reduction should be at the back

burner for now. It would be a disaster for us all, especially the future

generation.

The future generation will suffer more if unemployment

continues to grow at exponential rate. We could all be in a devastating financial

position ten years from now especially because of inflation. It is only people that have

money or good credit that can purchase houses. Nowadays, most

of us do not even have the money to live or get basic essential goods and

talk less of buying a house, which supposed to be our biggest investment

in our lifetime.

"EQUAL RIGHTS AND JUSTICE FOR ALL PEOPLE"

14

Should a President Be a Political expert?

I

do not really expect my president to be a *political science* expert,
although it helps to have ideas or experience in politics; but to be
a guru of politics sounds like a very good con man specialized in
politicking. So, it's not important because I experienced some
things
when I was in undergraduate school as a zoology (biology)
major. I did
not care much about the philosophy of politics but was
interested in
good leadership, which I was unfortunately deprived of in my
country
of origin.
Sorry! I did not mention earlier that I am duo-citizen of the
United States of America and my country of origin. Before,
I got my United States citizenship, I used to refer to myself as a
legal alien
but my friend objected to the term "alien." She said it sounds as
if you are
from the planet Mars, like those aliens from outer space with big
heads
and small, tiny round eyes protruding from the forehead; so,
taking to her
advise then I used the term permanent resident, to be politically
correct.
So, the reason why I gave up on people with majors in
philosophy

and political science. Maybe, I was just biased because I was a Science

student. When I was studying at the University of Lagos

for my bachelor's degree, normally after classes, I went back to the

dormitory and later downstairs to pick up some snacks at the cafeteria.

I used to see group of students and from their conversations I assumed

they were political science majors at my college if not all of them in that

group were political science majors, I guessed most of them were. All they

talked or had heated arguments about was philosophy of politics—topics

like political ideology of Mussolini; radical political ideologies like

anarchists, socialists, communists, Marxists, fascists; the advantages

and disadvantages of M. L. king's peaceful protest; why Nelson Mandela

"EQUAL RIGHTS AND JUSTICE FOR ALL PEOPLE"

15

should become the next South African president, atrocities of Hitler, and

so on and so forth.

I found some of those controversies or arguments interesting, but

majority of them were just too confusing, and eventually I got fed up

hanging around to hear more of those. There were too many unresolved

issues, and my thinking then was to get some resolved conclusions.

For example, what should be the solution to some of those political

problems? And none was forthcoming.

Don't blame me, I was a *zoology* (biology) major student and was

discouraged mainly because I studied some insects and other animals

with small brains but had natural order in their colonies compared to

us human beings (Homo *sapiens).* So, to me, most of the theories of

those talking heads then and especially nowadays on TV never resolved

anything but confusion.

Most of their audience cannot even comprehend their point of

argument: when you are dealing with the *masses,* you should put that

into consideration that not everybody is well read to understand your

point of view, so try to simplify things to really educate the masses.

Sometimes you must frame some sentences so the masses can comprehend better and avoid confusion. So, my president doesn't have

to be a political science expert.

It was so irritating on how some people were picking on Sarah Palin

(the vice-presidential candidate for the Republicans in the 2008 election).

Although, I was not into the Republican stand on most issues then, but

it was so depressing to me the way she was being treated; it was like

mental and emotional abuse. Most of those people talking I bet did not

know better. If she was that stupid and ignorant, she would never qualify

to be the governor of Alaska, USA. Some people said she was at the

right place at the right time, so Palin's abusers may have to wait for that

chance to be at the right place at the right time probably till eternity.

"EQUAL RIGHTS AND JUSTICE FOR ALL PEOPLE"

16

The President and education

hen people try to put down presidents or people in general as per
their education level, I find it offensive because honestly speaking,

I believe in good education *if* you let school go *through you* and not
just *go through school.* If you go to school and you cannot apply yourself,
that to me is a mere waste of time and money. Most philosophers in the
days of old did not really attend the conventional schools; they read
books and improved their thinking faculty. Nowadays, with the new age
of technology, you can study online; and if you apply yourself, you will
do better than most people that attended the conventional schools.

So don't tell me how the former President Bush is bad with some
pronunciation, how Sarah Palin reportedly said she can see Russia from
her backyard, that Dan Quayle was not a smart vice president, or most
African presidents did not get a college degree. We tend to bring down
and focus too much on people's weaknesses and never appreciate other
good qualities they have. Yes! I read Bill Gates was a college dropout, but
he has the money to hire thousands with master's and doctoral degrees.

And the same goes for LeBron James. It was a big discussion
before, when he was going to the National Basketball
Association (NBA)
from high school, that it was not good for the NBA to allow
players direct
from high school. And the same for Kobe Bryant. What college
degree
has to do with playing for the NBA? Some people that Oprah
Winfrey did
not have a college degree... She is one of the best in her business
and has
business IQ higher than most of us. All these people, especially
women, are
applying their skill sets in so many avenues; and we should all
appreciate
what they are doing for our societies.
Generally, we frustrate our women presidential candidates. As
men
we should think back as far as elementary school; we used to
think we
"EQUAL RIGHTS AND JUSTICE FOR ALL PEOPLE"

W

17

were having fun abusing women mentally by intimidation, if not physically, as

bullies. A friend of mine argued that boys bully boys, and some girls

bully other girls too, but you think of the ratio in later scenarios, it was

minute compared to boys intimidating girls.

I could recollect when I was in the sixth grade, we were in geography

class, and during a quiz, our teacher asked for the definition of "mirage"

or what causes a mirage in the desert. And a girl raised up her hand when

most of us did not have any response to that question. Most of

us were trying so hard not to have direct eye contact with the teacher

because some of the teachers just point to any of the pupil at random,

and if you missed the answer, you might be punished.

Her answer was so accurate and direct, explaining a "Mirage" as human

imagination of seeing a pool of water far away in the desert and which is not

a pool of water but the sun's rays reflecting on the sand dune at

a particular angle. But from far away, it looks like a pool of water.

And this was how she gave her definition of a mirage: "A mirage is

the effect of the sun *chining* on the sand dune in the desert and far away

you think it's a pool of water." Although none of us, especially the boys

in that class, knew the right answer to the definition of a
"Mirage"; but just
to make that *smart* girl feel low, we continuously picked on her
after that
class and till the end of our eighth grade before we all moved on
to the grammar school (high school). And that was a long time
ago, but
I still remember that incident as if it was yesterday. We used to
call her
"Sun chining" because of the way she pronounced "shining" as
chining,
and later we nicknamed her as "Chining face."
Thinking back, as boys I realized we used to try to put girls down
one
way or the other even when they were better off in the class, and
there was always a *double standard* between males and females.
When I
was in elementary school, I would never allow my mom to apply
lotion
on my face to avoid the other boys tagging me as "shining face"
or that
I'd look like a woman. It was a big insult in my school for other
boys to
say, "You behave or talk like a girl." And we (men) continued all
the bias
and abuses of the female gender even as grown men. I learned
wayback
that, women generally mature faster than men. A woman of
twenty-one
years of age thinks like a thirty-one-year-old man (grown man).
Apart from the current survey results that more women

are getting better skills and more advance education than men, *but*

"EQUAL RIGHTS AND JUSTICE FOR ALL PEOPLE"

18

women were offered fewer managerial positions. I ran into a lady in the

elevator in my apartment complex. I said hello and introduced myself,

and she was warm and friendly too and told me her name was Angelica;

then I gave her my business card in anticipation to get hers too. I paused

for a second, but she was not giving me back her business card in return.

We got off from the elevator, and it so happened she was going toward

the parking deck too.

She was so accommodating and seemed like a very nice person,

and we continued our conversation. So, I asked, "What do you do for

a living?" And she replied she had a bachelor's degree in economics

and master's degree in English and that she had a part-time job

and a temporary job in her field of studies but with no prospect of

becoming permanent because the company she was working for had a

freeze on hiring full-time workers because of the way things were going

with the global economy.

So, she decided to go for a more advanced degree; she was

on the way to meet with an admissions officer for the PhD program.

That was impressive, although I did not ask her how old she was, but probably she was in her mid or late twenties. She was so beautiful and

professional—great personality. I walked her to her car and said good

luck on the job search and the meeting with an admissions officer for

her PhD program.

I got to my car and tried to start my car but no luck, I was so disturbed

because then I had to call some of my clients and cancel appointments,

and I was planning to travel soon, so I had to do a lot with my committed

assignments and projects before my travel. While I was still going

through all these thoughts, I saw on my car's side mirror somebody was

coming towards my car, and I looked back and realized it was

Angelica. So, I told her, "I thought you left already."

But she said she had noticed while she was passing by my car that it

seemed I was having problem starting my car, because she was looking

to wave and say, "Good-bye!" But I was so consumed trying to crank

up my car. Angelica suggested I probably needed to jumpstart my car,

but I told her that I had a similar problem with my car a couple of days

ago, and the people gave me a new battery for free because I still had a

warranty on that battery.

So, I was wondering what the problem could be. I tried to start the car

again, and fortunately it started. I was relieved, but I knew my car had

a major electrical problem. Angelica smiled and left, and I was on my

"EQUAL RIGHTS AND JUSTICE FOR ALL PEOPLE"

19

way to my appointments too but was running a little bit late for the first

appointment. Fortunately, there was no major traffic delay, so I made it,

but still puzzled why my car would not start.

So, I decided I would go and buy the ignition switch and find a

roadside mechanic to fix that for cheap instead of going to the car dealer

for diagnosis. I was always skeptical of dealing with car dealers because I

assume they will charge me an arm and a leg; and to fulfill my personally

imposed austerity measures to stay afloat during the bad global economy,

then I had rather go the cheap route. Big mistake, because I ended up

spending a lot more than what I should have paid the dealer to check my

car and pinpointed the problem instead of my guesswork, which resulted

in me buying unnecessary parts. Unfortunately, they told me I could

not return them because they were electrical parts, once installed in my

car—so I have been stuck with them.

I met Angelica again at the parking deck when I got back home later

that day—what a coincidence! It was as if we had planned to meet again

at that time. I was delighted to see her again; then she asked if I took my car for diagnosis at the dealers to find the real problem. But I did

not know her that well, so I just told her I would be going tomorrow.

I knew I was not going to do that but instead meet with my roadside

mechanic as planned and install the ignition switch; I had just ordered.

I was curious, so I asked her where she was from and that she looks like an associate of mine, Kathy. Jokingly I said, "I guess she might be your twin sister."

But she replied, "I don't have a twin sister, and I'm from here," and

asked why I thought she was from another country. I said because of her

facial features, her light brown skin and of course, the beautiful, shining

black hair that was so long, up to almost to her waistline. She giggled,

smiled, and said, "Thanks for the compliments."

She had no accent for me to be in the position to guess where she was originally from. But before I got into that, she said to be specific,

she was born in New York; but her parents were from Brazil and Italy

and that they migrated to the United States in the 1970s.

I knew she was curious too about where I was from originally, and

she said, "I know you are not from here, so where are you originally

from?"

I smiled and asked her to guess at least from my thick accent, and she

guessed right, and I was shocked because I thought she would probably

"EQUAL RIGHTS AND JUSTICE FOR ALL PEOPLE"

20

guess the right continent but not my country of origin. Then I asked

how the meeting was with the admissions officer for her PhD admission

process, and she said her chance was fifty-fifty and that although her

grade point average (GPA) was 3.9, she was a straight A student but

unfortunately had a B in one of her courses.

I was so impressed—3.9 out of 4.0 GPA. So, I asked why she thought

her chance was fifty-fifty, and she said that was from the feedback she

got from the admissions officer, that since she was not interested in

getting a student loan because she feared accumulating more

debts because she still owed some student loans. She was scared to add

more, especially with the state of the global economy; again, she could

not secure a permanent job now.

Then I asked her what about grants and scholarships for education. I

stressed that because for those she did not have to pay them back. But she

replied that according to the admissions officer, the scholarships and grants

were not guaranteed as ever for students that had good GPA, especially

for women, because more women are going back to school than ever and I showed her the PhD admissions in the past three years; and

it was 100 percent, 90 percent, and 100 percent respectively of women

in the PhD programs compared to men. She said she was stunned to see

that kind of statistics of the yearly enrollment of women compared to

men and that she explained further that statistics were not just for that

school but nationwide.

So that was one of the major reasons it would be so difficult for more

women to qualify because it was already saturated, and she did not see

the trend changing anytime soon—more women getting advanced skills

and better education to meet the demands of the new millennium.

I was listening to a program on the radio, *Between the Lines,* and

the host was interviewing Karin Slaughter, a bestselling author. And

she said, "When you educate a woman, you educate the whole family,"

and when "we respect and honor women, everything falls into place."

I come from a country that the people think if you don't have a

college degree, you are seen as a second-class citizen, and we used to

joke around when I was in college and call those with less education

"No Future Ambition" (NFA). I visited my country a couple of years

"EQUAL RIGHTS AND JUSTICE FOR ALL PEOPLE"

21

ago, and most of those people we tagged as NFA were doing
better financially. I assumed most of them applied themselves.
My country had tons of people with master's and doctoral degrees,
and we failed to apply the skills to make that country better, one of the
many reasons we are still referred to as underdeveloped country (Third
World country) because after independence, most Third World countries
remained as nations of consumers despite the abundant natural resources
in most of those countries. This response was unbelievable—when one
of the former presidents of one of those countries, when asked about his
poor performance in his two terms as a president, he answered, "You
people elected me as president, and you did not expect me to build you
good roads, to provide you with clean drinking water, and uninterrupted
water and power supply. Although I know the Constitution allows just
two terms, but if you allow me to run for the third term, then I will find
solutions to these problems."
Don't get me wrong. Education is the key to many doors of
opportunities. They say *knowledge is power,* and I recommend you read

at least a book every other month. To me it is a way to develop your

thinking ability, and you can use them to make good things happen if

you apply them in the right manner. People go to the gym to develop

their muscles and strength; studying and acquiring knowledge is a

way to improve the brain—knowledge is power. And our imagination

and awareness could help us all make this world a better place. Imagine what

would become of our world when we start electing women as presidents

worldwide.

"Imagination is more important than knowledge. Knowledge is limited.

Imagination encircles the world."

—Albert Einstein (1879-1955)

Most people know where they belong, but like I mentioned earlier

in this book, I'm still sitting on the fence. Or can I be classified as

an "Undecided voter" once I'm ready to participate in one of the most

important civic rights for my country. Then I would find out if I am extreme

left, left, moderate, right, or extreme right.

22

I think being moderate is good. *But* I still have reservations as per being a moderate.

Also moderates can belong to any party, which is like being decisive about the agendas and not about a political party to vote for.

Political Categories: "Left," "Moderate," and "Right"

<<< "Extreme left"—"Left"—"Moderate"—"Right"—"Extreme right" >>>

I prefer undecided voters because it seems to me you are trying to

make a scientific or educational decisions on substantial issues and the

proposed positive agendas based on what you think will be beneficial

to others, especially the common people (the masses) before you cast

your vote. Although the undecided could be a chameleon too; I think

I should remain on the fence (Undecided voter). It is always better to be

an informed voter. To learn how to make better choices when electing

our leaders.

23

Women Can Make things simple and more effective

I

am about to share some things I experienced and learned from
women when I was in school. Somebody told me that it might be
mere coincidence, but it happened several times. So, to me, once the
probability of an occurrence is high; in science we assume it is not mere
coincidence.
I was in graduate school, and in most of the courses we formed teams.
in my team, there were two women and four men. During our project
compilation, I asked all the men how we should write the definition of
a computer, and most of us including myself got so technical, and why?
Just to show off what we knew. Since we were graduate students
(Master's degree in information technology), we thought we should not
sound so elementary during our presentation, and we kept on making up
complicated definitions that would never make sense to the masses. If we
included those kinds of definitions in our publication for non-information
technology people to read, I knew they would get so confused.

One of the ladies in my team suggested we should write the definition

as simply as possible, so others could understand and apply this knowledge.

So, her definition from what she read when she was in high school was:

"*A computer is a device that accepts input, processes data, stores data*

and produces output." And we asked her, **what are the main functions of a**

computer was. Well, she said they were already in the definition she just

gave us; and that would be *input, process, store,* **and** *output*.

I got back home after that team meeting and was kind of perplexed,

although I knew this simple definition of a computer too. But as a man and with

24

an advance degree in IT, I thought that was too simple a definition. I spent

almost four hours the previous night before that meeting to come up with

a more complicated definition of a computer. Women have some natural

gifts to resolve matters, and I got into an argument with a friend about

the Samson story in the Holy Book, about how a woman brought him to

his knees with all his power. But his main point of argument was kind of

obscene to me and one of the many mistakes we are making as men.

We tend to see women as only useful for a particular purpose, but I

think they have better intuition about so many things if we allow them

to participate and not the barbaric notation that the place of the woman

is in the kitchen. One of the many mistakes the women make too is by

thinking we should oversee most things from time immemorial.

Somebody mentioned the Roman Empire ruled the world and how many

women participated in the many wars the Roman Empire won and made

them the world power then. Yes! They won many wars and spread that

empire all over *their* world, but who were taking care of the soldiers

home when they were at war? And maybe if they had allowed a woman
to be their leader, probably they could have been satisfied and not been
at war all the time to conquer more and more cities out of greed.

Most women leaders would be more compassionate and would not
continue fighting unjust wars. The current world situations because
men continuously being in charge is not really working, and things
are not getting better; it's like the law of diminishing returns.
So maybe we should allow the women to take over the driver's seat.

As men we are just too aggressive. For instance, in most wars the
warlords are mainly men. This group of people stirs problems with the
notion that their opposition's intent is politically based, but in reality, their
foremost actions are based on criminal intent. I wish we could all apply
the traffic laws to the way we live, and maybe that could eliminate all
these chaotic situations. Traffic laws especially in the developed countries
are awesome. If the traffic light is red, you must stop. The amber light
means "get ready to stop," and green means go. Talk less of the other
numerous traffic signs we must follow to avoid confusion and be safe.

Come to think of it—my third month in the United States and the

traffic laws. I was so eager to start driving because I fell in love with the

beautiful city. The roads were nicely paved and well-constructed, with

"EQUAL RIGHTS AND JUSTICE FOR ALL PEOPLE"

25

traffic lights almost everywhere, and that kind of setup was like night

and day compared to my country of origin.

My uncle from one of these developed countries had visited my

Country of origin while I was still there and made a comment that it was as

if we were "driving inside a well" because of the bad roads. I thought

he was just being arrogant then, but now I am in a developed country, I

could comprehend what he was complaining about then.

I couldn't wait to experience the awesome driving experience and

also to drive around and see more of the beautiful city. I used some of

the money I brought from my hometown (Country of origin) to get a car for

less than $900. I used to call that Datsun 310 my "Jalopy." It ran well but

needed some professional paint job, but unfortunately, I had spent most of

my money already.

I was bent on doing the paint job myself, so I went to one of the Auto

stores to get ten cans of car spray paint and picked glossy black, my

favorite color. I got to my place—it was a room-a-house kind of living

arrangement, and this house had a big backyard. I assumed that house

was probably over hundred years old.

26

I finished painting my car and the next morning I got dressed to see more of

my beautiful city. I knew I had all my papers for the car, my driver's

license was current, and I was not speeding. So, I was just wondering

what the police officer was stopping me for.

He got off his motorbike and walked slowly toward me, and I noticed

he placed his hand on the radio attached to his shoulder. He greeted

me cordially, and I was shocked. A police officer talks to people nicely

here— "Innocent until proven guilty." I was surprised a police officer could

be that polite; I was not used to that kind of treatment in my hometown.

He asked me for my driver's license and insurance. I gave them to

him, and he said, "I will be right back," and asked me to sit tight in

my car. I was wondering why he was walking back and talking on the

radio attached to his shoulder pack. I went through a series of "maybe"

thoughts and concluded maybe I had just bought a stolen car. While I

was going through all these thoughts, I looked on my side mirror and

saw him coming toward my car again.

He said everything was all right but asked, "Who did your paint job for you?"

And I replied, "I did." He found that hilarious and said he

stopped me because he thought it was a stolen car. Then he smiled and left.

I was so relieved and continued my trip to the downtown; then

the unfortunate happened. I got to the downtown, then got a little bit

confused with the traffic light signal. It was showing a green arrow

pointing to go straight, but I thought because it was green, I could turn

right too. Although I had passed my traffic test theory on the computer

in flying colors, I couldn't know why I made that mistake turning right

instead of going straight as indicated by that traffic light arrow.

As soon as I made that turn, I saw a blue light flashing behind me

and I assumed again the police officer was asking for right-of-way

like the ambulances do. So, I parked, but I saw him parking directly

behind me. Then I knew I was in trouble. I sat calmly in my car, and I

thought he was stopping me too for the bad paint job; but he walked over

and asked for my driver's license and proof of my car insurance, and I

gave them to him.

He went back to his car for almost five minutes, and I saw him

walking toward my car again. He asked me, "Do you know why I stopped

you?" and I replied because of my bad paint job.

"EQUAL RIGHTS AND JUSTICE FOR ALL PEOPLE"

27

He smiled and said that was not the case but because I had made an

illegal turn, and I realized my mistake and told him I was sorry and that

I was new in the country. But he replied, "I bet they have traffic laws all

over the world." He paused for a second or two and said, "I will give you

a warning this time," and he left.

I was so relieved about not getting a ticket and kept on driving,

enjoying the downtown scenic views. Then I saw another blue light flashing

behind me but a little far back but continued to come toward me. I

slowed down, and he slowed down too; then I knew I had just committed

another traffic violation, but I was wondering what my offense could be

the second time. It was the same police officer, and he said, "You just

did the same thing I had just warned you about. I must write you a

ticket this time, and please pay more attention to those arrows."

Unfortunately, I got my first ticket, but I avoided getting another

ticket for so long, probably for about three years. It was not the "green

arrow" but a parking violation ticket. Sometimes I wondered, "Where

are the female police officers?" My friend thought it was because most

men are too aggressive, although the women would be in their
uniforms
    and everybody's supposed to respect that. But some people will
always
    try to take advantage of women, so they assign them to other
tasks and
    not the traffic unit.

28

Your View on Why a Woman should not Be a President

As a man, I don't want to be self-centered and chauvinistic as most
of my gender group operates, so I tried to get the point of few of
both genders: males and females. I was not disappointed finding
out
that most men think women are not qualified or capable of being
the
commander in chief and president of nations, especially the
developed
and well-advanced countries.
The reasons why? No substantial reasons but just the norms
of time immemorial, that physically and mentally, we men
assume
women are not capable to *shoulder* that kind of responsibility.
And I
asked what physique has got to do with being a president of a
nation, it's
not like tons of stones that you must pull around, and if so,
nowadays
there are so many inventions to move tons of stones. I'm not
trying
to be sarcastic talking about a nation as a stone, but sometimes
when
an argument seems unjustified and nothing really to quantify
people's
point of view, I think my argument and the point I was trying to
make
is appropriate.
What do you mean by women are not physical? There are

lots of women in most of the Developed World military, and majority are

performing their designated appointments and tasks. We men decided

what it is fit and not fit for women to do because of our stereotype as

per their strength. I bet it takes a lot of strength physically and mentally

to carry pregnancy for nine months. Talk less of the strenuous pain

during labor. As men we never experience this kind of stressful pain and

discomfort. All the things' women go through during the childbearing

"EQUAL RIGHTS AND JUSTICE FOR ALL PEOPLE"

29

period, they are still mentally strong and caring to nurture their baby to

become a productive citizen in most cases.

With all these qualities of women, I think they are qualified to be

presidents not only in the Third World nations but the developed nations.

I prefer to see that happen soon in one of the developed nations to really

show the whole world they are really qualified, and all of us should

support them because they have been there for us from time immemorial,

like the saying "Behind any successful man, there is a good woman

supporting him." This could be vice versa.

I discovered most women think they are not ready or qualified

too, which is so disappointing to hear from most women that being a

country's president is a man's job. Who says? It's just the norm that was

imposed on women's thinking from the beginning of time.

A lady associate of mine told me the other day, "Listen, I am a

woman, and I like the awareness you are trying to establish for all

both males and females to realize women are capable of this kind of

responsibility. But once a woman gets to that position of authority, her

whole demeanor changes."

I don't agree that should deprive women of that kind of achievement because we all go through changes, both women and men. I asked her,

"Have you heard of the midlife crisis men go through?" So, it is not only

women that go through changes, biological or emotional. We could all

see things are not really getting better globally, both financially and for

world peace, so what's next?

"Intuition will tell the thinking mind where to look next."

—Jonas Salk (1914-1995)

"EQUAL RIGHTS AND JUSTICE FOR ALL PEOPLE"

30

Are Women a Minority Group?

I could not comprehend why women are grouped as a *minority,* so

I decided to research the true meaning of minority. The definitions of

minority are below.

1. (a)

(b)

2. (a)

(b)

(c)

3.

The smaller in number of two groups forming a whole.

A group or party having less than a controlling number of votes.

A racial, religious, political, national, or other group thought to be different from the larger group of which it is part.

A group having little power or representation relative to other groups within a society.

A member of one of these groups.

Law: The state or period of being under legal age

(Source: yourdictionary.com)

These are basic definitions of being a minority, and women do not

fit into any of the groups except for 2. (b). In this case, we (men) denied

them to have the power and representation in all our political systems

worldwide.

So why do we tag women as minorities? Probably we think they are second-class, and they do not actually belong to our group, so to honor

them, and men being sarcastic, we decided to group them as minorities.

Women's population is higher than men's, and if we never denied them

"Equal rights and justice for all people"

31

of education and rights to vote, they will always be the majority; and in

democracy, the majority rules.

So, men are supposed to be the minority group, but we continuously

ruled from time immemorial; therefore, we assumed to be the *elites* and

the *oppressors* in societies worldwide. We could relate this kind of

situation to what happened in South Africa, Rwanda, and some other

countries for years before the majority (Women) finally came to power.

Since women have realized they are the majority group, and nowadays

women are getting better job skills and education compared to men.

women should start creating the awareness all over the world; and most

of the developed countries are civilized enough to eradicate oppression of

any sort. *It's about time* to give women the chance to be more involved in

politics.

To all the men in the world, the women need our help. There is a saying,

"Behind any successful man, there is a woman." So now, not to be

self-centered, we should revise that role and break the *invisible wall*

between the female and the male gender. The invisible wall has resulted in the superiority complex by men especially in the *political arena* and

has led to the recent discussion about which group is competent enough

to oversee the day-to-day activities in our societies. The *world is changing,* and we should all learn from the mistakes of the past, due

to ignorance. Creating either *invisible* or *physical* walls will never do

our societies any good, and we should all learn from the history of the

physical wall in Germany.

It is always better when we unite. The physical wall in Germany was

demolished in 1989, although between two to three billion dollars was

spent in the process of unifying Germany. But it was worth it because

we could all witness the advantages of unification of Germany, both

financially and for world peace. Germany was in the position to help

other European countries, especially during the global financial

crisis. Germany played the role of a "big brother" and being a big

brother could also be stressful sometimes because you are committed to

help. The same kind of role the United States has been playing forever by

helping and giving aid to the people of the world. When they demolished

that wall, Germany benefitted financially, better harmony between her people and global peace.

The world is changing; and to survive, we should all learn to adapt,

especially the male gender. Presidential appointments should be based

on merits and not the gender group. Nowadays more women should be

"Equal rights and justice for all people"

32

in the position of authority, especially in the developed countries. From

the beginning of time, we focused on and emphasized mainly men's

achievements, as if women just came into existence. Most of the brave

women and leaders in the past, e.g., Mary Slessor's achievements, the

women pilots and nurses in World War Two, great women scientists,

women inventors, women CEOs and top entrepreneurs.

"Equal rights and justice for all people"

33

Letter from the Common People

Common people worldwide

Political leaders/ Representatives Worldwide

Letter from the Common People

This is to our current and next generation of political leaders and representatives worldwide. Please sponsor programs and projects and

promote agendas that will be beneficial to the masses in our societies,

especially for our children, the elderly, and people that are physically or

mentally challenged. Nobody in these groups of fellow citizens should

be homeless or starving. They should be provided with affordable or

free health care services.

For the rest of us, please create jobs. We are ready to work and

prepared to improve our job skills to meet the demands of this millennium.

Hopefully soon, the more fortunate among us ("*Common people*") will start running small businesses that will eventually create

more jobs. No more wars because there is nothing like a good war.

We've had enough of this suffering amid abundant wealth.

—Voice of the Common People

"Equal rights and justice for all people"

34

Democracy and Fairness

T

he basic definition of democracy as I learned in my social science
class in elementary school was and still is, "*The government of the
people, by the people, and for the people*"—not the government of
men, by *men* and for *men,* as has been practiced from the
beginning of
time. I wish we could practice true democracy because I am sure
women
are people too.
A democratic government is explained as the primary source of
power for the common people; the common people can also
vote for and
elect their representatives—majority rules. A democratic
government
must also abide with the principles of *equal rights, equal
opportunities,*
and *unbiased treatment* for all.
In sports, when we have matches, there will always be a winner;
but
we talk about *playing a fair game* by abiding to the rules of the
game.
When your team wins, we all cheer for your team and
acknowledge
if it was a fair game or not. Although there is always bias,
especially
when we are on the opposing team. As an opposing team, we
always
find a reason or reasons why we should not have been beaten
(losers). In

every sport, there is always more than one person or just one team.

We could apply this same analogy to the female and male genders.

Let's assume politics is a game. The teams are, on one side, the women's

team; and the other team is the men's team. But the only team showing

up all the time is the men's team, and the women's team seldom shows

up. To be a fair game, we should give the women's team the opportunity

to show up and play all the time too, win or lose—that will be at least

fair enough.

"Equal rights and justice for all people"

35

Although some people argue we have video and computer games
for individuals, and they are fun games. Yes! Initially it could be
an
exciting fun game playing it by yourself (you beat yourself by
improving
your scores); but I bet after some time, because of human
nature—we
love competition—that game will eventually become boring.
And this
is from personal experience. *Sometimes you must be challenged to
improve in most endeavors.*
When you play against somebody, for example, in tennis, or for
instance, a football team playing against another team, it is
always
exciting because of the competition and improving individual
or team skills because of this competition and the will to win.
You will
always strive to be on top of your game. We could improve the
quality
of our politics by getting women more involved. Men leaders
might
eventually improve on how to govern and stop being
self-centered.
Naturally most of us like to support the underdogs in most
sporting
events, especially if we noticed that team was trying. It's true we
should enjoy sporting events for the fun of it. But sometimes we
all get
carried away with our emotion and always want our team to win
even

when we know the other team was better off, or some will say, "No

competition."

For instance, in 2009 LeBron James (one of the best players in

professional basketball in our lifetime) and the Cavaliers visited my

home team. They beat us to a pulp. I like LeBron James, but it

was so domineering in that series and continuously dunked on my home

team. I felt so bad to see my home team not really competing, and that got

me sick to my stomach—Yes! Some people will say it was just

a game, but sometimes it affects us from time to time to say the least. Mine

normally doesn't last for more than six hours, and I could be classified as

normal as per team solidarity, but some of us carry that too far.

Apart from my home team that year, my other favorite NBA team was the L.A.

Lakers. Kobe Bryant was the best of the best NBA pro players, especially during that season, I could recollect some tough matches especially with the to-be-beaten dynamic trio in Miami, Florida—the Miami Heat. That was my friend Dr. Henry's team, he could not comprehend anybody stopping his team, but I told him it would be better singing

"Equal rights and justice for all people"

36
"We Are the Champions" at the end of the finals.

I was kind of weary about the Lakers, but hopefully they will rise up

again, to the occasion. As for my home team, we needed more pieces

to make that puzzle complete, and solidarity is very important. So, try

as much as possible to support your home team. Come to think of it, we

all talk about the National Basketball Association (NBA) for men but

seldom mention the Women's National Basketball Association (WNBA)

as if they are not that important; and the sponsors are biased

too. Most of us can hardly name at least five WNBA teams. Even some

of us do not know the name of the WNBA team in our *state.* We are all

guilty of the *double standard,* and hopefully we could all start reckoning

with women better than ever and *not only* as our mothers, sisters, wives,

friends, and associates *but* to start giving them the equal opportunities

in our societies worldwide.

Facts: In a survey in 2010, there were more skilled women workers and

also, more women with advanced education than men but less managerial

positions compared to men. In fact, in the 1960s and 1970s, only 20 percent of women were in the workforce in the United States. And

could you believe, *1920* was the women's liberation in the United States,

a First World country and one of the most advanced countries in the

world. Although we still have a long way to go to acknowledge women's

achievements and their competence in our societies worldwide, to be

more effective we should all start the awareness now in this millennium,

especially in the developed countries; and eventually the developing

countries will catch up.

"Equal rights and justice for all people"

37

Not in our Generation

D

o you believe too that reoccurrence of women's presidency will not be

in our generation? Women's presidency in the developed world as a

continuous occurrence and not a once-in-a-blue-moon appointment.

Do you think this will not come to pass in our generation?

Remember Rome was not built in a day and not in our wildest

dream could we have imagined the possibility of electing the first black

president in one of the most developed countries in the world.

The effect of the computer era, the power of the Internet,

and all the latest electronic gadgets at our disposal nowadays have really

enhanced our communication power; and the whole world is turning

to one big village. So, it is easier for the masses to get and relay vital

information to one another, and all these have created better awareness.

This same logic could be applied to how we could help create the

awareness on giving the women the opportunity to hold one of these

high positions of authority. The women's presidency movement could

be embedded in our subconscious and eventually make it happen and

become reality.

I was in the library the other day, and this gentleman asked me

about the project I was working on. I was so delighted to show him my

manuscripts on trying to promote the awareness to start electing women

as presidents in the developed world and eventually in the future all over

the world. We were in the library; so to be civil, he whispered and

said, "Not in our generation."

I was not angry or disappointed because of his point of view, belief,

and ideology; but I was interested in making a few concise points for

him to go home and digest. Maybe I would be in the position to share my

"Equal rights and justice for all people "

38

point of view with that gentleman, so I asked him if we could step out

of the library for a few minutes, and hopefully he would comprehend

better. We spent almost an hour talking about issues.

I love to have intelligent conversation, and I never get angry.

Reluctantly I agreed on some of his points of arguments; we were

both consumed with this great debate, at the same time listening to

one another's disagreement and agreement. Finally, we both agreed

to disagree on some of the substantial issues affecting the chances of

a women's presidency.

The major issue was that gender equality has been suppressed

for time immemorial, and women have being brainwashed about the

limitations of their role in politics. We are not talking about the women

who rules countries because of royal inheritance or

ceremonial monarchs, e.g. Queen Margrethe II of Denmark, Queen

Beatrix of Netherlands, or Queen Elizabeth II of the United Kingdom

of Great Britain and Northern Ireland. We are talking about women who are

appointed through a *democratic election process* to the position of presidency.

I did enjoy the conversation. We exchanged email addresses.

Recently I got an email from him, and he mentioned that it was a good

move to create the awareness but that it might happen in our lifetime
but not any time soon. I somehow agreed on maybe "not any time
soon" but in our lifetime. Come to think of it, most men are
too aggressive; and don't get me wrong, it's good to be aggressive to
an extent—I think it's our gene makeup. However, this kind of approach is not
applicable to solve most of our encounters in life.
"Some people argue for electing women as presidents especially
in the developed world but not in our generation. Then, maybe:
I suggest you
search on the internet and read on... "How the *Rwandan women came to power*
to dominate the political process in that country.
I laid more emphasis on electing women as presidents in the
developed countries in *this* millennium, but I was surprised when I read
an article on how the Rwandan women dominate the political scene in
Rwanda after the civil war that led to the genocide of 1994. According to
the *Human Rights Watch* estimate, between five hundred thousand and
one million people were killed, and that was estimated to be 20 percent
of their total population. The war started because of the longstanding
ethnic condition and tension between the minority *Tutsi* and the majority
Hutu people.

"Equal rights and justice for all people"

39

Most of their men were killed, so now the women took control of

their government. Now they (the women) are in the position of authority

to keep their country going after the unfortunate situation. The latest

Rwanda quota system allowed more women to be in politics, and actually

half of their parliament is women. As I read, most of these women were

performing well, but it is sad that we only give women the chance to

rule most of the time only at extreme situations, especially when we are

left with no other choice. And the effectiveness of the Rwandan women

has promoted women in decision-making positions worldwide.

"No one can make you feel inferior without your consent."

—Eleanor Roosevelt (1884-1962)

"Equal rights and justice for all people"

40

Men's Birthright to Be President

o you think it is one of the *laws of nature* for men to be presidents?

Not, because depriving the women the rights to be presidents

especially in the developed world are *manmade laws,* which is also

known as "good laws" (good laws are directly opposite laws of nature).

But these good laws are *bad* laws as we all see in politics.

For example, women's liberation occurred in the United States, a developed and superpower country, in 1920, in the United States, women

were not allowed to vote for so long due to one of the *manmade laws.*

One of the laws of nature: What goes up must come down—the law

of gravity, as most of us learned in physics.

Force = Mass multiplied by Acceleration or F = MA is another law

of nature.

So, I got into an argument with my uncle, who happened to be well-educated, a professor of physics; he was so adamant and concluded

that writing anything to make people aware of the role women would

play as presidents of nations will never hold water because that's the

way things were set up in life. Men have major roles to play in politics,

and he believed women have some limited roles too but not as the "main

man."

I corrected him on that phrase "main man"; rather, he could have said

"Main person." My uncle should learn more and be aware of politically

correct words and statements. Not until I started working on this project,

I had never thought or realized most people especially men see a woman

as a nonfactor in most things. I can see they perceive this gender as not

"Equal rights and justice for all people"

D

41

equal. I can see why we deprived them of getting good education in the

past: some in those days (the past) thought it was a waste of time and money to send a woman to school, especially in most Third World

countries. As we can all see nowadays, because people became more

enlightened and started sending their daughters to school, the women

are doing better than most men.

Generally speaking, and to be gender-specific, we men are more violent and defensive than women. But "an eye for an eye" will never

solve most problems; many times, cool heads and patience prevail. I heard

on the radio the other day in a scenario for example, when somebody

smacks a man on the head, at that moment he might not be ready to fight

back. *But* later he will grudge on himself on why he did not fight back.

In another scenario, a man went for a walk at the park and suddenly

heard a cracking sound or offensive noise. He would look to see where

the danger was coming from, then keep on going, *but* for a woman in

the same kind of scenario, her first instinct would be to run away from

that danger.

"Equal rights and justice for all people"

42

Women Political Leaders in the Past and Present

I

am not an historian but researching the women political leaders in
the past and present, I was astonished by their accomplishments. You
can do your own research too; then you might be surprised by these
women's abilities and achievements—especially most of us men that
think women are a kind of second-class. This is not like a competition of
the genders but coming to reality that it is about time to put the women
in the driver's seat since things are not really getting better in the world,
as we can all see.

Women Political Leaders—Historical and Current

(Source: Information Please Database, http://www.infoplease.com)

The following table lists the current and historical female political leaders of the countries of the world, according to country name, woman's name, political title, and years in power, including Queen Elizabeth I, Benazir Bhutto, Margaret Thatcher, and more.

"Equal rights and justice for all people"

43

"Equal rights and justice for all people"

Queen Elizabeth

Benazir Bhutto

Country	Name	Reign
Angola	Queen Nzingha	1582-1663
Argentina	President Cristina Fernandez de Kirchner	2007–Present
Argentina	President Isabel Perón	1974–1976
Lesser Armenia	Queen Zabel	1219–1226
Bahamas	Governor-General Dame Ivy Dumont	2001–2005
Bangladesh	Prime Minister Khaleda Zia	1991–1996, 2001–2006
Bangladesh	Prime Minister Sheikh Hasina Wajed	1996–2001
Barbados	Governor-general Dame Nita Barrow	1990–1995
Belize	Governor-general Dame Minita Gordon	1981–1993
Bermuda	Premier Pamela Gordon	1997–1998
Bermuda	Premier Jennifer Smith	1998–2003
Bolivia	Prime Minister Lidia Gueiler	1979–1980
Brazil	Queen Maria I	1815–1816
Brazil	Empress Isabel (regent)	1871–1872, 1876–1877, 1887–1888
Burundi	Prime Minister Sylvie Kinigi	1993–1994
Byzantium (Roman Empire)	Empress Theodora	1055–1056
Cambodia	Queen Ang Mey	1835–1840, 1844–1845
Cambodia	Queen Kossamak (joint ruler)	1955–1960
Canada	Governor-general Jeanne Sauvé	1984–1990
Canada	Prime Minister Kim Campbell	1993 (4 months)
Canada	Governor-general Adrienne Clarkson	1999–2005
Canada	Governor-general Michaëlle Jean	2005–
Central African Republic	Prime Minister Elizabeth Domitien	1974–1976

Cherokee Nation	Wilma Mankiller	1985–1995
Chile	President Michelle Bachelet	2006–
China	Empress Wu Chao	655–705
China	Dowager Empress Tsu-Hsi	1861–1908
China	Dowager Empress Longyu	1911–1912
Denmark	Queen Margaret I	1387–1412
Denmark	Queen Margrethe II	1972–present
Dominica	Prime Minister Mary Eugenia Charles	1980–1995
Easter Island	Paramount Chief Koreto Puakurunga	1868–1869?
Easter Island	Paramount Chief Carolina	1869?–1888?
Egypt	Queen Hatshepsut	1501–1498 B.C.
Egypt	Queen Tiye	1415–1340 B.C.
Egypt	Queen Nefertiti	1372–1350 B.C.
Egypt	Queen Nefertari	1292–1225 B.C.
Egypt	Queen Arsinoe II (joint ruler)	279–270 B.C.
Egypt	Queen Berenice	81–80 B.C.
Egypt	Queen Cleopatra VII	51–30 B.C.
Ethiopia	Empress Candace	332 B.C.
Ethiopia	Empress Zaudita	1916–1930
Faeroe Islands	Prime Minister Marita Petersen	1993–1994
Finland	President Tarja Halonen	2000–present
Finland	Prime Minister Anneli Jäätteenmäki	2003 (2 months)
France	Prime Minister Edith Cresson	1991–1992
Georgia	Queen Tamara	1184–1212
Germany	Chancellor Angela Merkel	2005–
Ghana	Queen Mother Yaa Asantewa	1863-1923
Great Britain	Boadicea, Queen of the Iceni	c. 26–61
Great Britain	Queen Jane (Lady Jane Grey)	1553 (9 days)
Great Britain	Queen Mary I	1553–1558

Great Britain	Queen Elizabeth I	1558–1603
Great Britain	Queen Mary II (joint ruler)	1689–1702
Great Britain	Queen Anne	1702–1714
Great Britain	Queen Victoria	1837–1901
Great Britain	Queen Elizabeth II	1952–present
Great Britain	Prime Minister Margaret Thatcher	1979–1990
Grenada	Governor Dame Hilda Louisa Bynoe	1967–1972
Guyana	Prime Minister Janet Jagan	1997
Guyana	President Janet Jagan	1997–1999
Haiti	Provisional President Ertha Pascal-Trouillot	1990, 1991
Haiti	Prime Minister Claudette Werleigh	1995–1996
Hawaii	Queen Liliuokalani	1891–1893
Hungary	Queen Mary	1382–1387
Hungary	Queen Elizabeth	1439–1440
Hungary	Queen Maria Theresa	1740–1780
Iceland	President Vigdis Finnbogadóttir	1980–1996
Iceland	Prime Minister Johanna Sigurdardottir	2009–present
India	Prime Minister Indira Gandhi	1966–1977, 1980–1984
Indonesia	President Megawati Sukarnoputri	2001–2004
Ireland	President Mary Robinson	1990–1997
Ireland	President Mary McAleese	1997–present
Israel and Judah	Queen Athaliah	842–837 B.C.
Israel	Prime Minister Golda Meir	1969–1974
Italy	Queen Theodelinda	590
Italy	Queen Joanna I of Naples	1343–1381
Italy	Queen Maria of Sicily	1377–1402
Italy	Queen Joanna II of Naples	1414–1435
Jamaica	Prime Minister Portia Simpson Miller	2006–

Japan	Empress Suiko Tenno	593–628
Japan	Empress Kogyoku	642–645
Japan	Empress Jito	686–697
Japan	Empress Gemmyo	703–724
Japan	Empress Koken (abdicated)	749–758
Japan	Empress Shotuku-Koken	764–770
Japan	Empress Toshi-ko	1762–1771
Latvia	President Vaira Vike-Freiberga	1999–present
Lesotho	Paramount Chief 'Mantsebo Amelia 'Matsaba Sempe	1941–1960
Liberia	President Ellen Johnson-Sirleaf	2006–
Lithuania	Prime Minister Kazimiera Prunskiene	1990–1991
Luxembourg	Grand Duchess Marie Anne de Bragance (regent)	1908–1912
Luxembourg	Grand Duchess Marie-Adélaïde	1912–1919
Luxembourg	Grand Duchess Charlotte	1919–1964
Madagascar	Queen Ranavalona I	1828–1861
Madagascar	Queen Rasoaherina	1863–1868
Madagascar	Queen Ranavalona II	1868–1883
Madagascar	Queen Ranavalona III (deposed)	1883–1897
Maldives	Sultan Amina Rani Kilagefanu	1757–1759
Malta	President Agatha Barbara	1982–1987
Micronesia	High Commissioner of Trust Territory of the Pacific Islands Janet J. McCoy	1981–1986
Monaco	Princess Louise-Hippolyte	1731
Netherlands	Queen Wilhelmina (abdicated)	1890–1948
Netherlands	Queen Juliana	1948–1980
Netherlands	Queen Beatrix	1980–present
Netherlands Antilles	Prime Minister Lucinda da Costa Gomez-Matheeuws	1977

Netherlands Antilles	Prime Minister Maria Liberia-Peters	1984–1986, 1988–1993
Netherlands Antilles	Prime Minister Susanne Camelia-Romer	1993, 1998–1999
Netherlands Antilles	Prime Minister Mirna Louisa-Godett	2003–2004
New Caledonia	President Marie-Noëlle Thémereau	2004–present
New Zealand	Governor-general Dame Catherine Tizard	1990–1996
New Zealand	Governor-general Dame Silvia Cartwright	2001–2006
New Zealand	Prime Minister Jenny Shipley	1997–1999
New Zealand	Prime Minister Helen Clark	1999–present
New Zealand (Maori community)	Queen Te Ata-i Rangi-Kahu Koroki Te Rata Mahuta Tawhiao Potatau Te Wherowhero	1966–2006
Nicaragua	President Violeta Barriosde Chamorro	1990–1997
Nigeria	Queen Amina of Zaria	1588-1589
Norway	Queen Margaret	1387–1412
Norway	Prime Minister Gro Harlem Brundtlandt	1981, 1986–1989, 1990–1996
Pakistan	Prime Minister Benazir Bhutto	1988–1990, 1993–1996
Panama	President Mireya Moscoso	1999–2004
Peru	Prime Minister Beatriz Merino	2003 (6 months)
Philippines	President Maria Corazon Aquino	1986–1992
Philippines	President Gloria Macapagal-Arroyo	2001–present
Poland	Queen Hedwige	1384–1399
Poland	Premier Hanna Suchocka	1992–1993
Portugal	Queen Maria I	1777–1816
Portugal	Queen Maria II	1826–1828, 1834–1853

Portugal	Prime Minister Maria de Lourdes Pintasilgo	1979 (149 days)
Roman Empire	Empress Irene	797–802
Russia	Empress Catherine I	1725–1727
Russia	Empress Anna Ivanovna	1730–1740
Russia	Empress Elizabeth Petrovna	1741–1762
Russia	Empress Catherine II (The Great)	1762–1796
Rwanda	Prime Minister Agathe Uwilingiyimana	1993–1994
St. Lucia	Governor-General Dame Pearlette Louisy	1997–present
São Tomé and Príncipe	Prime Minister Maria das Neves	2002–2004
São Tomé and Príncipe	Prime Minister Maria do Carmo Silveira	2005–present
Scotland	Queen Mary Stuart (executed)	1542–1567
Seminole Nation	Betty Mae Jumper	1960–1969
Senegal	Mame Madior Boye	2001–2002
Sheba	Queen Makeda	960 B.C.
Spain	Queen Dona Urraca	1109–1126
Spain	Queen Juana I	1274–1307
Spain	Queen Juana II	1328–1349
Spain	Queen Dona Blanca	1425–1441
Spain	Queen Isabella I (joint ruler)	1474–1504
Spain	Queen Catalina de Albret	1481–1512
Spain	Queen Isabella II	1833–1868

Source: Information Please® Database, © 2007 Pearson Education, Inc.
http://www.infoplease.com

48

Woman pilot in WW2
Mary Slessor

Sow the Seeds of Victory!
   Mary McAleese
   Helen Clark
   Angela Merkel
   Hillary Rodham Clinton
   Ellen Johnson-Sirleaf
   Nancy Pelosi
"Equal rights and justice for all people"

49

Cristina Fernandez de Kirchner

Sarah Palin

Tarja Kaarina Halonen

2009 NATO Summit, France

Aung San Suu Kyi

Women World Leaders (Pictures, Sources: Wikimedia Commons. http://

commons.wikimedia.org. Please see *Photo Credit* section for more information)

Although America does have many women politicians, most of our political leaders today are men. The 2006 World Economic Forum

Gender Gap Report found that the U.S. ranked 66th out of all nations for

women's Political Empowerment, our lowest score out of many sections

in the report.

This could be due to the many challenges women face when they enter the political arena. According to research done by the White

House Project and its affiliates, voters tend to think that women are

less effective and tough than men. This puts women candidates at a

disadvantage before the campaigning even begins.

"Equal rights and justice for all people"

50

Having a proven record of past political gains is very important aspect of campaigning, yet voters tend to think women are less likely to have proven records just judging on the fact that they are women.

Women in politics also have the difficult task of maintaining a specific appearance. They can't appear "too casual or too glamorous," whereas men can throw on a suit and look professional. The physical appearance of women politicians tends to overshadow their effectiveness as a candidate.

I think we need more women in positions of power in our country.

This will give younger girls positive role models and specific female influences on their goals. If our country continues to label women as ineffective and 'soft,' younger generations will pick up on this trend and the cycle of a mostly male political arena will continue.

What do you guys think?

—By Jacqui K

The article above said it all, so *it's about time* we start creating the *awareness* about women presidents, appointing women as political leaders and increase the presence and involvement of women in political arenas worldwide.

"Equal rights and justice for all people"

51

Women Becoming Breadwinners

I

t was summer of 2007. After a long day at work, on my way home around

6:00 p.m., I decided to stop over at the grocery store to get some food

and toiletries. Normally I do not enjoy shopping at this time of the day

because the lines are always too long, and the shopping aisles are always

as if you are on the highway during the rush hour traffic, bumping into

people, people bumping into you. You are continuously saying "excuse

me" so many times, to be polite. Do you notice too that there are more

people in the frozen food aisle because nowadays everybody is always

in a hurry and prefer to get something to microwave?

I waited for my turn to pick up my favorite frozen food too. I joined

the long line to get to the cashier, then remembered I forgot to get my ice

cream. Reluctantly I went back to that most busy aisle (the frozen food

section) and spent more time the second time around because it seems

we all got so confused choosing which ice cream flavor in our favorite brand and nowadays, which one is on sale regardless of our preferred

brand. For me I tried as much as possible to be frugal, not being cheap

but self-imposed personal austerity measure to keep up with the current

global economy. The producers of most of these products were not really

helping us out because they had so many varieties of these products, so

we got confused deciding what to get and what not. *Time is money.*

I wondered why they cannot just make it simple, like ice cream

flavors of vanilla, chocolate, or strawberry. Finally, I got the things I

wanted in order of preference, then decided to come back later that night

probably around 11:00 p.m. or midnight, my favorite grocery shopping

time. I looked at my watch. Wow! I had been shopping for almost an hour,

"Equal rights and justice for all people"

52

initially I had planned to just rush in and out, so my initial estimation

was at most not more than twenty minutes. I was on the check-out line

and out of boredom, my eyes were wandering all over the store. Then

getting frustrated to see why the line was not moving, I bent my head a

little bit to see if the line was moving at all. Now I realized there was a

man in front of our line.

It was his turn to pay, but I could see he was saying something to

the cashier: although I could not hear their conversation or argument,

from his body language I assumed he was having some trouble with the

cashier. I wondered what was happening. So contemplating if I should

return my items to the aisles, I picked them up from and come back

another day, preferably at night as I was thinking earlier.

People on our line started whispering what was going on. Now we all

knew what the problem was. He was trying to pay with a personal check.

Unfortunately, the machine used for verifying the check was unable to

verify his check or was malfunctioning. Anyway, he said he did not have

cash or a debit or credit card and insisted that the cashier should get him her supervisor or manager and that he needed the phone number for

their home office (headquarters).

Apparently, we were all stuck, and to switch lines meant you have to go back to the tail end. But luckily, he gave up, threw his hands up

out of frustration, and walked out—what a relief, and the line started

crawling again. The store manager was out earlier to resolve the check verification problem, but since the unhappy customer had left,

one of the ladies on my line suggested that the manager should open

more cashier stations during the rush hours; but he just shook his head

in acknowledgment of her suggestion. I still shop in the same store, and

nothing has changed with their rush hour delay.

Nowadays women are becoming breadwinners, and as men we must

not see this as an insult for not being "man enough." Man enough?

Actually, I just corrected my uncle about using politically correct phrases

and not terms like "main man," "man enough," etc. We all used the

term "sitting at home mom" for ages. That means women that take care

of their children and household while their partner or husband goes to

work.

In this millennium, *the table has turned* probably because of the worldwide financial crisis. Women are getting good jobs with better

"Equal rights and justice for all people"

53

income due to their skills set as reported in one of the recent surveys. The

percentage of highly skilled women was higher than men. So now we

have lots of "sitting at home dads," and there is nothing wrong with that.

So, we (men) should swallow our pride and go with the flow. The world

is changing, and we must be able to adapt.

Yes! The "sitting at home dad" situation is acceptable in the developed

world, but that will be taboo in most of the Third World countries because

of our (men) egos. Thinking back while I was in elementary school,

even as a young boy I found it awkward seeing my neighbor's dad at

home when we got back from school. I was used to seeing the women

at home, I used to think then that women were not supposed to go out

and work but only to take care of her children. Most of the women did

some petty trades at home or some places very close to home. Some of

the women used to do some weaving artwork. Some of them used to go

to the market to trade, normally they were home already before we got

back from school. So, to see that man (my neighbor's dad) at home when we got back from school was strange.

I asked my mom out of curiosity why that man never at work during the

daytime, and she scolded me to stop being nosy. Luckily for me, that same man came

later that day to our house to chitchat with my dad. I overheard him

telling my dad about having some financial problem to get his car fixed.

Unfortunately, that was the car he used as a taxicab; but eventually he

got his taxicab fixed.

It is true women are more skilled than men nowadays; they are

getting most of the skilled positions that are more in demand in this

millennium. My friend said, "This is the end of men," out of frustration

because of women's advance of careers, but I did not believe that.

I had read a book about the "end of men." I was kind of paranoid

and worried when I first saw the title of that book, not until I read it. It

was about how women are getting more skilled and more. As men we

will never go into extinction. That was my thought when I came across

that book, but we must learn how to *coexist* with ourselves and the other

gender. Most of us have this view that women should not be in charge or

control of things; we have this superiority complex.

For instance, when I first had a woman as my manager, initially I felt uncomfortable and defensive about most of her approaches; but all my

female managers or superiors were the best. Even one of them

"Equal rights and justice for all people"

54

recommended me to her boss to be considered for promotion as one

of the store's manager. I know it might be difficult to change all men's

views as per women's leadership capability, but with better awareness,

most of us will eventually believe this and join the bandwagon in the

crusade for women's equality and see why they are overdue for the

position of leadership, especially as presidents of countries.

"Equal rights and justice for all people"

55

We Could Apply a scientific Approach

I

talked about, argued, and commented on why we should start electing

women as presidents in the developed world. You might have read in

the previous topics in this book why I suggested it in the developed

world now. Scientific advancement has changed the manner we

virtualized the world, the manner we do things, and more. So nowadays

our thinking must be scientific, we should do away with the stigma of

the presidential position being mainly for men.

Have you ever wondered how the airplanes fly so high with all the

added cargo and people in them? The airplanes defy the law of gravity

due to advanced technology and scientific innovations. We can see

around us, even if we don't have one, all the new electronic gadgets,

and the evolution into the computer era. So our thinking and the way we

perceive things should change too; we are no longer in the Stone Age.

Scientific approach—here's a very good personal experience

I am about to share with you. I ordered a package from a company; they sent me the wrong package. I was disappointed, but luckily that company was local, so I decided to drive down to pick up the right package. On my arrival at their office, I was greeted cordially by the receptionist. Luckily for me, while I was still complaining about getting the wrong package, the frustration of probably not meeting the deadline of the project I needed that package for.

She (the receptionist) gazed out the window and said, "Here comes the

supervisor in charge of the department that sent out the wrong package,

and he will be able to resolve the problem." Again, she apologized for

the inconvenience.

"Equal rights and justice for all people"

56

The supervisor came in, and he was also friendly and professional

too. Just before I uttered a word about the wrong package, the secretary

told him what had happened. He was furious, sent for the dispatcher

person that had processed my order, and asked him to be "scientific"

next time when sending out orders.

He explained calmly to the dispatcher that the items were categorized

and color-coded so there was no excuse why anybody should make a

mistake of sending out wrong orders and that 99.9 percent of the time,

it must be right. *Nobody is perfect,* I assumed 0.1 percent human error

in their company could happen to anybody, and I was just unfortunate

falling into that category.

In fairness, as I overheard their conversation, the dispatcher was new

in that company. Maybe he did not get a good sleep the previous night

or had other personal problems—who knows? But I hope he did not lose

his job. They finally gave me the right order, and I was just lucky enough

to meet the deadline for my project.

The scientific approach should be the *new world order* since we are becoming more advanced in our thinking. We should be flexible enough

to consider women as our counterparts, associates, and *equals*. It's about

time to give them the chance, long overdue especially in the developed

world. In science we follow a sequence (the scientific approach) of

events before anything can become law.

Hypothesis → Theories → Law

And we can apply this scientific approach here too to women presidency as

Awareness → Justification → Appointment as president

The term "scientific approach" is sometimes also coined as

"Systematic analysis and procedure." I was working for a manufacturing

company; then that company decided to increase their productivity

efficiency and safety. So, they hired some experts to come and show us

the methods of achieving that. It worked, but unfortunately that

company laid off some workers after that process of increasing their

productivity because it became apparent that some of the workers needed

"Equal rights and justice for all people"

57

some other basic skills to accomplish how the new procedures were set up.

It was six months later, after the new efficient and more productive manufacturing processes, that they then hired more skilled workers.

As we could all see for example, in the United States, the economic downturn has resulted into massive layoffs. I heard in the news that unemployment was 9.6 percent national average; some states are still over 10 percent and even as high as 16 percent in some races in the United States, because skilled employees are a necessity especially in this computer era and advanced technologies. You can research this too yourself. In a recent survey, they found there were more skilled women in the job market than men. With the unemployment as high as 9.6 percent, some careers (skilled jobs) cannot even find enough qualified people to fill these positions.

Another survey reported that some other skilled jobs, e.g., carpentry, plumbing, and electricians were in demand despite the real estate bubble.

Normally parents preferred to send their children to the four-year colleges, and most of the kids feel that it's not cool being a carpenter or

that plumbing is a dirty job.

I felt the same too while growing up. My parents and sisters wanted

me to be a medical doctor, which was never my interest, and I never

did achieve that either. I wish I had the guts to tell my folks then that I

was not interested in pursuing that, that I'd rather be an artist. Drawing,

painting, and design were my primary interests in my high school days,

but I was forced or talked to major in science because they thought it

was cool to be a medical doctor.

Some parents want their children to be lawyers, engineers,

accountants, and some other cool professions. Nowadays, the

cool professions are forensic investigator, software engineer, brain

surgeon, stockbroker, etc. To be realistic, we cannot all be in these

careers, but getting the right skills especially in the jobs that are in

demand could impact our life and the economy in general. In a latest

survey, the ratio of professionally skilled women is higher than men, so

women are filling up all these skilled positions but in lower managerial

positions.

"Equal rights and justice for all people"

58

Nowadays most medical related jobs are in demand, especially registered nurses. We used to think being a registered nurse was for women, but recently more men are going to nursing schools and other paramedical studies than ever. Women are more professionally skilled nowadays than men, so the preferred gender to be in the position for presidency should be women, apart from their ability to *nurture* and also disciplined to be *patient* compared to the male gender.

"Equal rights and justice for all people"

59

Women Wearing the
Pants in the Family

his is no longer about ladies wearing designer jeans, tight polyester
silk pants or a pair of short shorts (hot pants), all for fashion. In
this generation, that is no longer a fashion statement *but* women
nowadays are becoming the breadwinners of most families all
over the world probably because of the global economic
situation. In one
of the latest surveys, women are better off than men financially
because
they outnumber men in professional skills, so they are in demand
more
in the job market.

I visited my country of origin (*Hometown*) not too long ago; I
was
surprised to see that women are becoming the breadwinners in
some families.

I called my niece to tell her I was in town, could not wait to see
her—ten
years! That was quite a long time. She was excited knowing I was
in
town. I could sense the excitement in her voice too. Yes! Ten
years that were long enough. I couldn't believe that I stayed away
for that long—how time flies.

We arranged to meet after work. I asked her about how the
husband
and her children were doing. Reluctantly, with a deep breath, she
said,

"Just fine."
From the tone of her voice, I knew she was going through

some hard times. I asked her why she sounded so low because I used

to know her personality; she was a fun-loving person, smart, and hardworking. So, I pressed further on why she was not happy.

T

131

60

Then she opened up and told me that her husband was laid off over

a year ago, and that he had not been successful getting another job. Then

I realized what she had been going through. She was the only one catering for her family. Her children were still in elementary school,

and they normally go to the babysitter for a couple of hours after school;

then she was obliged to pick them up. Unfortunately, the one and only

car they had was having some major engine problem. They did not have

enough money to fix it, so public transportation was her only way out.

But she spent hours at the bus stop because of the *inefficient* public

transportation system in my hometown.

She said once she got home, she was already worn-out because of the hectic life in my hometown. Her next agenda at home was to prepare

dinner for her family, make sure the children did their homework, then

get ready for work and get the children ready for school the next day before going to bed. She sounded like a superwoman to me because

I could not imagine the kind of stress she was going through to survive.

Talk less of living life. Then I pondered after she told me about her very busy schedule. I was amazed because something was missing in her

story.

I understood what she was going through, but what was missing in

that picture was the husband. So, I asked her, "You mentioned earlier

that your husband was laid off from his job." I understood he was job

hunting, but I could not comprehend why he was not helping with

picking up the children and at least help them with their homework to

give her some free time to relax and *exhale* before cooking dinner for

them.

I was shocked to hear her response to my question, that "the husband

is the head of the family." Maybe because I had been away for so long

that I should remember that's not our culture for men to help with

housework. I could not believe that was her response. Yes! I understood

our culture was not applicable to the way things are now in this

age. The world is changing, and it's better we adapt to most of these

changes.

Then I asked her where the husband was. Job hunting? She replied,

"At the Internet café." I was pleased to hear that, assuming he
was *online* applying for jobs.

So, I asked her, "Which Internet café?" Then she gave me the name

and the direction to the café. Fortunately, it was close to where I was

"Equal rights and justice for all people"

61

staying; in fact, that café was in the same estate (subdivision), less than

twenty minutes' walk.

It was around 5:00 p.m. in my hometown, and that would be around

11:00 a.m. in the United States, where I had just come from. The weather

was so beautiful; it was sunny with less humidity but a little bit hot for

me since it was winter at the country I came from. Then I freshened

up. I was kind of fatigued because of the jet lag and also my flight was

delayed for almost seven hours at the Amsterdam airport during transit

in the process of changing my flight to my destination.

Stepping out of the house, I realized my outfit was not meant for that

kind of weather in my hometown, so I went back in to change into more

comfortable attire. I put on my jeans and a nice short-sleeve T-shirt. I got

to the Internet café located just a stone's throw from the main gate to our

subdivision (estate). The place was well organized, a decent space for an

Internet café had about six computer stations.

I noticed some people just hanging out, having chitchat, but it was

not too crowded; I spotted my brother-in-law in one of the computers stations. Although he looked a little bit different from when I had seen him the last time—to be precise, almost ten years ago, at their wedding.

On their wedding day, he was clean shaven, looking like "A million dollars" and due to the wedding day euphoria—we all plan to look our best on our wedding day. But at the café that day, he looked so tired and desperate.

He was not well-kept. At my first glance, I hesitated if that was the right person because then, he had grown facial hair. He was wearing faded jeans and a dull white T-shirt. I instantly noticed the change in his appearance that was probably due to financial stress, and maybe he was feeling less of himself. Well, I knew that was him, so I went straight to his station and tapped him lightly on the shoulder.

He looked up at me, and for a second or two, the expression on his face was as if he had seen a ghost. He finally recognized me, jumped up from his chair, yelled my nickname at the top of his voice, and gave me a big hug. Then we stepped out of the café to engage in chitchat.

We had a lot to talk about. Wow! I screamed, "You look a lot different from the last time we met at your wedding—facial hair and a little bit

darker in complexion," and he responded that I gained some weight too

but that I was still looking fresh and healthy.

"Equal rights and justice for all people"

62

We exchanged pleasantries and talked about the weather for a second.

I knew his situation already from the conversation I had with his wife

and not to beat around the bushes, I asked him about the progress with

the job search. His response was that he was into Yahoo! now. I actually

thought Yahoo! just gave him a job or something to do with promoting

Yahoo! business ventures in my hometown, but *no!*

He was doing Yahoo! not as a legitimate information technology or

marketing career, *but* as a "419 venture" (fraud)! A scam artist, stealing

people's money online or sending out bogus emails, telling those that are

greedy enough to fall for them, generally uninformed new entrepreneurs,

especially rich old folks how they can get rich quick.

I was disappointed and told him the repercussions, "Even if

you make money through that kind of *scam,* you might not enjoy the

kind of good life you anticipated." Then I told the wife too about the

whole scenario later that day after dinner. We all had a very intelligent

conversation. He said I should listen carefully so I could understand why

he had decided to embark on that kind of venture as a con man, that it was out of desperation. He preferred to do that than armed robbery, but

to me, it was kind of similar. It was just that armed robbery was

more violent and real, so I should say scamming people online should

be termed "virtual armed robbery" (VAR), because in the later scenario

you will be using the Internet as a weapon and not a gun but basically

still destroying people's lives.

He said he was well-read, with a bachelor's degree in economics, and

a second bachelor's degree in computer science. When he could not get a

job, he decided to go for the master's degree in business administration,

with the thought that he was putting himself in better position to qualify

for most job prospects. But all was in vain because businesses actually

stopped hiring most especially because of the global economic hardship.

And when they do they give jobs, it was to only people they know, and

that was the practice in our hometown.

But I corrected him on that, because nowadays companies in the

developed countries do the same, it's all about who you know—you get

jobs most of the time only when you have connections. And he continued

to explain that as a man, you need money to support your family. Anything less than that, he stressed, means he was not really pulling his weight

"Equal rights and justice for all people"

63

because eventually your wife will conclude you are not capable to maintain

and be the head of the household.

I did not totally agree on the assumption that a man should be

the only one to make money to take care of his family or shoulder all

the responsibilities, but it is true in my culture the man must be the

breadwinner. He thinks women should take over and run our governments

worldwide. I told him it might be a great challenge for us to start creating

this awareness about the better role women will play in our political

system worldwide, most especially in the developed countries.

Fortunately, I succeeded in changing his mind and he now works

for a telecommunication company in my hometown, also in a better

position to help my niece in supporting their family. I was so impressed.

He was intelligent and eloquent. I was glad we crossed paths again and

fortunately had that conversation; he was just about to go on the wrong

path in search for quick money and might have wasted all those great

skills and talent in search of quick money out of frustration.

The world is changing. I think it's better to always adapt to these changes,

in case your wife is in a better position financially and you, the husband, not being idle or lazy to earn a living but unfortunately jobless, and it's

just so difficult to find any source of income legally. You should at least

find the time to help or relieve your wife of the other duties in the house.

And, if you are fortunate to have an understanding partner, eventually

you will secure a job and be able to support your family too.

But the greatest mistake, finding an easy way out of your financial

woes, might end up being a time bomb and not always the best option. I'm

not playing the devil's advocate. Majority of the people in my hometown

are smart and hardworking. Unfortunately, we always have leaders

that are never compassionate, self-centered and always indulging in

mismanagement and embezzlement.

Most of my people are well-read, and getting a bachelor's degree is

a standard or norm. We are not born con men or crooks as most people

in the world perceive us, but the terrible situation our government put

us make most people in that part of the world so desperate to the extent

of engaging in criminal ventures for survival. I do not condone this kind

of criminal activities, but I promise things will change for the better in

Africa and for all the oppressed people in the world. Help is on the way.

It's all about awareness.

"Equal rights and justice for all people"

64

Scam Email Sample
Please be careful of fraud!

—Original Message— [I removed the contact information to protect the innocent]

From: *Scam Kingsman*

To: undisclosed recipients.

Sent: Tue, Jun 22, 2024, 9:55 pm

Subject: YOU HAVE A PACKAGE WITH *XXXXXX* [a well-established courier company]

XXXXXX Courier Express

0000 Fake Ave

Xo 12345

VTB

Tel: 123 456 7890

Dear Friend,

This is to inform you that there is a parcel containing a Bank draft of 900,000 USD in your name.

My name is Scam Kingsman, Delivery manager *XxxXx* Office in Scam Avenue, Xo. I have been waiting for you since to come down here to pick your Bank Draft but never heard from you. Well, be informed that your parcel has been here for the past one month from a Compensation and Finance House in *FakeCountry* but your address is incorrect and hence we could not reach you to deliver the package so it has remained here in our office. We hereby await your current address.

Now to enable us to the delivery of your parcel containing the bank draft, you are hereby required to forward your contact information as stated below.

(1) FULL NAME . . ..

(2) ADDRESS . . ..

"Equal rights and justice for all people"

65

(3) COUNTRY . . ..
(4) PRIVATE TEL . . ..

Note also that upon the receipt of your contact information above, we will proceed with the delivery of your parcel to you after conditions are met and you sending to us your valid delivery address as true owner of package.

Contact me at our delivery department immediately with your contact information and I will update you on how soon we will deliver your parcel.

Here is my contact detail:

Contact: *Scam Kingsman*

Address: *Xxxxx Courier Scam Pl.*

0000 *Fake Ave*

Xo 12345,

VTB

Tel: *123 456 7890*

Email: *fraudman@getalife.uc*

Phone: *123 4670000*

Expecting your response and your contact confirmation soon and to the above office.

Please note that you have to call me before or after sending me an email.

Yours sincerely,

Scam Kingsman

(Source: From my friend's email inbox, forwarded to me)

"Equal rights and justice for all people"

66

Listed below are some of the Fraud Protection Services around world, and their services are *free.*

National Crime Prevention Council in the United States of America:

www.ncpc.org

German Forum for Crime Prevention (DFK) in Germany: www.kriminalpraevention.de

European Crime Prevention Network in Europe: www.eucpn.org

Cybercrime Prevention Organization in Africa: *www.*

thenewnewinternet.com and visit *www.allafrica.com* and search for

cybercrime prevention.

Russia and Switzerland jointly fight against cybercrime: *www. silobreaker.com*

Cybercrime prevention in China: *www.chinadaily.com.cn*

France's National Cybercrime Investigation Unit: O.C.L.C.T.I.C.

L'Office Central de Lutte conte la Criminalité liée aux Technologies de

l'Information et *www.4law.co.il*

You can also log on Cyber Crime in **Spain** and other countries: *www.*

cybercrimeupdates.blogspot.com

Most wanted cybercriminals and more: *www.ccmostwanted.com*

"Equal rights and justice for all people"

67

You could have also noticed ironically the young generation of men is

dropping their pants as a fashion statement. Probably not a coincidence,

men-to-be are dropping their pants as a fashion statement; but

psychologically they are about to give these pants back to the women

(the future world leaders). Think about this, and you too can see a lot of

telltale signs of things to come and actually coming to pass. Women are

becoming breadwinners.

"Equal rights and justice for all people"

68

How Bad Decisions Affect the Masses

W

e cannot blame the government for using monetary or fiscal
policies in general to stabilize the economy. That was one of the
things we elected them for, to take care of business. So there was
nothing wrong when the federal government spent *billions* of
dollars to
save the "too big to fail" financial institutions.
But most of them, especially the banks, did not use the money
they were given for the appropriate purposes, for instance, as
loans
for most people that were qualified to start small businesses that
could
have help reduced the unemployment so more money in
circulation.
The government spent all that money to bail out those
institutions in
anticipation that they will use it to create more jobs (loans
availability
for small businesses), and those small businesses could have hired
more
people. But instead those companies continued to build their
liquidity.
Some of the economic experts think the government should
focus
more on reducing the deficit. My economics is elementary, but
I understand a little bit about the law of supply and demand.
Literally,
the higher the demand, the lower the supply, and vice versa. We
can

apply this law to buying and selling also in a way to the high global

unemployment. You can manufacture and produce goods *but* nobody

will buy because they were unemployed, so no income to invest or buy.

Even some people are deprived of buying basic goods for their families

because of the bad global economy.

As I mentioned earlier, I am not an expert in economics, so my

understanding of the gross domestic product (GDP) is also elementary

as it could be, as per how the GDP determines if a country is in recession

or not. But even if the GDP calculations indicated that we were no more

"Equal rights and justice for all people"

69

in recession, I understood that. But because the country was no more

in recession did not justify that the people in that country are out of

recession because there is *individual* recession. Ask the masses that are

unemployed. Then maybe you could comprehend better the suffering

people are going through; and if drastic action is not taken, most of us

in this generation will be in recession for our lifetime.

Yes! The country can also be out of recession but could be at a state

of slow economic recovery because of high unemployment, which could

continue in that trend for years if the government does not take drastic

action to create more jobs.

I think our political leaders worldwide especially in the developed

countries should stop toying around with the state of the deficit as a

political device to get them elected. Leave the deficit alone for the time

being and encourage the government to use some of the money to create

jobs to drastically lower the percentage of unemployment. Some will

argue that our children in the future generation will be heavily taxed to reduce or eliminate the deficit. But don't you think that generation will

even suffer more if this trend of unemployment continues to grow the

way it is now.

Sometimes extreme situations require extreme measures. By creating

more jobs, the masses will be comfortable to spend. I think that trend will

simultaneously improve the economy, but since I am not an economics

expert, probably I could be wrong. So, this is just a suggestion.

In any society, the establishment and stabilization of the middle

class is the key for economic growth. Initially at the beginning of the

recent world financial meltdown, the initial coping mechanism for the

middle class was by borrowing from the banks. I heard on a radio talk

show, to be precise on WSB in the United States, from one my favorite

talk show hosts, although I didn't buy most of his ideologies. But when

you listen to him; it might be educating as per his point of view on some

political issues. Most of my associates could not believe I find his show

interesting, and recently during one of his shows, he mentioned that the

politically correct word for borrowing is now "stimulus," as stated by

one of his correspondences.

The middle class maxed out their credit cards and refinanced their

mortgages to stay afloat. But unfortunately, the banks finally got into

financial trouble too. So the majority of the banks and the well-established

"Equal rights and justice for all people"

70

financial companies were bailed out by the government, especially in

the developed countries. "Then: "It was to avoid the total financial collapse

of those countries or eventually the global financial meltdown, because the

developed countries support the rest of the world both financially

and with other aid.

For instance, in the United States, companies such as Fannie Mae,

AIG, Goldman Sachs, and most of the big banks that were tagged as

"Too big to fail" companies were all bailed out by the federal government

with robust economic stimulus packages. But these "Too big to fail"

companies or financial institutes were unwilling to make loans. They

decided to use that stimulus package to improve their liquidity instead

of making loans to assist small businesses. They also denied the people

some important loans that could have helped because of the layoffs,

which affected all the working classes. Hence people started getting

lower credit scores or bad credit. As a result of that trend, most people

were not qualified to get loans. At the same time, the banks and other financial institutes elevated the criteria to qualify for loans, thus making

it impossible for a very high percentage of people (the masses).

The actions of these financial institutions were another recipe for

total financial meltdown, and we might end up in double-dip recession

if the gross domestic product (GDP) growth slides back to negative after

a quarter.

If any country continues in the path of eliminating the middle class,

then the class setup in that society will result in either poor or rich.

That's one of the ingredients for chaos, as we all see that happening

in most of the underdeveloped countries, where the people, especially

the supposed leaders, engage in embezzlement of the highest order,

nepotism, bribery, and corruption. Even the Third world countries that

had the natural and human resources to become financially secured

were becoming the worst countries on the face of earth. Their natural

resources that were supposed to make some of these underdeveloped

countries better were becoming a curse. Sometimes I wish most

Third World countries should learn, practice democracy, and learn how

the democratic process (true democracy) works.

I know some will argue that the democratically advanced countries

are not perfect either, *but* it is like comparing an A-grade candidate to

an F-grade candidate. In this scenario, the latter are the Third World

"Equal rights and justice for all people"

71

countries (underdeveloped countries). Another havoc in eliminating the

middle class—then the *rich* has most of the finance and power to buy

outside influence like other foreign governments or groups, which could

eventually destabilize the ways of life of the people, for instance, their

freedom and dependence on foreign aid to survive.

In the underdeveloped countries, men are always in power too,

like every part of the world. But they (men) did greater damage to the

financial state of these Third World countries; the masses suffered most.

So, when all these men can clean up the mess and allow the masses

to start electing true leaders through the democratic process. Not until

some of these groups of people stop imposing themselves by rigging

elections against the will of the people, then maybe they will be ready for

women's presidency. In a recent survey among all the underdeveloped

or sometimes categorized as Third World countries, only China (China

is not only getting better but will probably become number one in the

near future as reported by some financial analysts) and also India were the countries that improved their production and financial gains with

the loans they got from the International Monetary Fund (IMF), the

financial aid from the developed countries for the millennium growth

project.

"Equal rights and justice for all people"

72

Austerity Measures and Your Money

ctually, I just thought about another way to save money or spend
less. It might sound ridiculous. But after a family friend told me
about their piggy bank and how they used the money they collected
from their piggy bank to do some things for their family at the
end of
the year, especially to get gifts and some basic goods for the
holidays, I
was surprised.

I went to a store to get my own piggy bank; and at the store, I
met
Mr. John, one of the customer service personnel at that store. I
asked if they
carried piggy banks. He was so delighted to show me and took
me
to the aisle. I noticed that he was a very good salesperson, and
apart from
the professional etiquette, he was so friendly too. He asked if I
needed the
piggy bank for my child; he assumed I had one, and I did not
have to go
through the story of my life about still being single and no
children.

So, I just replied that I needed the piggy bank for myself. He gave
me
a look as if he was saying, "What do you need that for?" But
before he
could alter a word, I told him I needed that to start saving. I
explained

how I could start saving some loose change and even a dollar from time

to time tucked into my piggy bank, which could become useful at the

end of the year, assuming I started at the beginning of the year. Then he

nodded with approval, that might help too with the state of

the global economy.

Now Mr. John and I started talking politics. It was kind of a slow day

for them at that store, I sensed he was really in the mood to talk

politics and the suffering of the masses. Although I had an appointment

with a client, but that was couple of hours away, so I was willing to talk

politics too.

"Equal rights and justice for all people"

A

73

He lamented that he had been working for the same company at
that store for over ten years. But for the past three years, their
sales were going down, and he wished the government would
find other
means of creating jobs for the common people (the masses) so
they
will have money to spend and that will help to jumpstart the
economy too. He said "this *man*" was really trying his best
because the
"Other *man*" really messed up things. He meant mismanaged
the country's capital, and he gave me this analogy.
"Imagine a house in disarray, junk everywhere, unwashed dishes
in
the sink for weeks. People that live in that house leave their trash
all
over the place, and nobody was willing to even take the trash out
for
so long. So, imagine you arrived in the same house and decided
to get
rid of the entire bad situation. It will take you days to straighten
up
things before it becomes a decent environment to live in. Talk
less of
putting some decorations to make that house look beautiful, you
might
also have to do the interior paint job too. So that was what this
man was
going through."
I understood Mr. John's point of view, and that was a perfect
analogy. At the beginning of a sentence or sometimes halfway
through,

Mr. John kept on saying, "Look here! Look here!" I guessed that was

his way to make me pay more attention to what he was saying, although

I was. But to be honest, my mind was wandering sometimes during our

conversation.

How I wish one of our representatives or senators could be there and

hear the lament of the common people, but unfortunately that was just

my fantasy because they don't even shop in that kind of store. And when

they organize a forum like a town hall meeting, 95 percent of the seats

are filled up with their paid foot soldiers to cause disruption, to make

sure, that the agenda that will benefit, make things better for the common

people are blocked and never to be addressed. Most of our political

leaders worldwide are self-centered, especially in the underdeveloped

countries. So, if they win the election or reelection and continue

their good life that is their foremost personal agenda, I hope they live

and let us live. And that's all we ask.

While we were talking, this other gentleman joined us. I was carried

away with the conversation and did not remember to introduce myself.

But I assumed he knew Mr. John. Probably a regular customer at that

"Equal rights and justice for all people"

74

store, he had his input on the conversation too; but he said something,

and I wasn't sure if he was serious or probably it was just a joke. He had

the kind of look as if as he was serious, but I couldn't still believe he

said, "The real estate bubble was caused by the federal government and

that it was a conspiracy by the federal government to give everybody

free houses, but that program backfired."

I couldn't believe he said that; that statement sounded so ridiculous.

I could not comprehend where he got that kind of information from. I

was just about to tell him to stop the joke, but he got a call, then said

he had to go. That was a call from the temporary agency, and he needed

to make the money, so he walked toward the front door of the store in a

hurry. I tried to get his attention because I thought he was just clowning

about the *free houses.*

But he looked back just before exiting and said, "I am serious, and

you will find out is the truth soon." But to me that was

ridiculous. I was still at that store checking if I could get other things

to buy, and Mr. John just moved some items from the aisle to the back room. Then I saw him walking toward me again.

He said, "Look here, you see that guy that just left was a supervisor at

one of the call centers down the road from here. He said his department

was dissolved, and their job was outsourced." I believed him

because that guy was eloquent and had the personality of a leader.

Mr. John suggested that the government should have imposed

austerity measures on us, but I told him that kind of action will never

be implemented in most developed countries especially because of the

people's freedom and liberty. But I think they were doing that indirectly

because their agendas and programs were not really helping the

underprivileged (common people); the rich were getting richer, the

poor getting poorer, and the middle class was about to become history.

The common people are going through austerity by spending

less and buying goods that are necessary. There is a saying, "Cut your

coat according to your size."

I had just started my own austerity measures. For instance, going

to the movies was my favorite pastime, but I could not afford paying

ten dollars or more for a movie, and unfortunately there are no more

two-dollar theaters. I could have gone to get a dollar chocolate bar from the dollar store, and that would have saved me lots of money even with

my date. I used to show my student ID to get a discount at the movie

"Equal rights and justice for all people"

75

theaters, but I lost it and could not get another ID since I was no more

a student.

My date chastised me once for using my student ID for

discounts, but I told her I would be a student for life. Since I could

not afford going to the movies as ever, I started entertaining myself by

listening to the radio. Normally I just scan through until I find something

interesting.

One night I got so lucky to get one radio station. The host

was telling a story. It was so funny and entertaining, so I continued

listening. I learned during one of their intermissions that the radio

program was on the National Public Radio (NPR). It was *A Prairie Home

Companion with Garrison Keillor.* Garrison Keillor and Bill Cosby are

the best storytellers of our time.

Another thing that could have improved my self-imposed austerity

measures, and I would have probably saved a lot of money, was if the

government would eliminate income tax and instead introduce fair tax.

Then I would be able to keep all my income and pay tax only on things

I purchased. That would be so good if the government could implement that, but I wondered how the government make money to run the system.

So I asked somebody the other day, and she referred me to the Fair Tax

website to read more about it.

Some of my friends did not really care much about my austerity

measures because they feel it could be inconvenient. They did not like

buying cheap stuff. They said they will never buy most of those cheap

stuff, but things they tagged as cheap stuff worked for me. Most

of the time, they could not even tell if I had bought a particular item

from their high-end stores or my cheap stores. I understood there were

some items you must buy from those high-end stores and some others

to buy in the other stores, especially to save money when there is an

economic crisis.

My associate asked me to buy some items for her. Initially she liked

the things I bought for her. She was shocked when I told her the amount

but later discovered I bought one item she requested from

that same store: then she was not too happy because she said the quality

was not as good as the ones from the regular grocery stores. I agreed

that some items (things) should be purchased at the high-end or regular grocery stores, but you could save a lot of money buying other things at

the cheap stores or buy generic products (store brands) sometimes.

"Equal rights and justice for all people"

76

I looked at my watch. It was 5:00 p.m.; I could not believe we had been talking for a little over thirty minutes. Then Mr. John was just about to change our conversation about the good, the bad, and the ugly of politics to why he thinks the world is coming to an end because there were telltale signs. I doubt that and was not really interested in that kind of conversation. I think as common people, when things are bad, some of us try to console ourselves that the world is coming to an end. The rich and the affluent people never want to believe that because they think they are already living in heaven on earth.

Mr. John said this is the beginning of the end of *Homo sapiens,* and I told him jokingly that the new and would-be intelligent species in that new world might have better attributes, like being compassionate, not self-centered, exhibiting empathy, with better sense of judgment, ability to coexist and living a chemical-free life. On a more serious note, I think all these chemicals around us in our foods are affecting our brains and subsequently reducing our ability to comprehend better or think straight, to realize what are real and what are not.

I hope Mr. John's forecast about the world coming to an end was just an illusion because I don't want those aliens we make up on our TV shows with their big heads and tiny purple eyes to be the ones to take over the *new* world, after we all *evaporated* from the surface of this earth. But if that is the case, I think they will not be friendly. We all judge others, so pardon me for exhibiting one of my *Homo sapiens* (human beings) attributes because what we think is beautiful as human beings might be ugly to them.

As they say, beauty is in the eye of the beholder. But I'm certain the aliens will be driving 100 percent electric cars, so they don't have to depend on foreign oil to survive, and their new world will be green with little or no pollution. Importing crude oil is becoming more and more difficult mainly because of the international politics, policies and demands by the main crude oil producers, the logistics, and more. The aliens will probably be better money managers so their true democratic government will not have to give them stimulus packages. If they did, their government will lay down rules on how the stimulus must be spent or implemented, especially some percentage of that as loans to help the common people in their new world.

"Equal rights and justice for all people"

77

Another school of thought about the world coming to an end created

another scenario that maybe our world is not actually coming to an end

but instead invaded by those aliens from others planet. Although we

created these characters in our TV shows and movies as fiction, they

might be real and waiting to invade the planet Earth.

Hopefully the latter is not true because I find those aliens so arrogant.

and from their demeanor, they are not afraid or intimidated by

human beings. At least we are polished enough to address a congregation

by starting with the phrase, "Ladies and gentlemen." But in most of the

movies, those aliens address their folks as "my people," and you can not

even differentiate their gender. At least our women are beautiful, but as

I mentioned earlier in this book, beauty is in the eye of the beholder.

I could not get the kind of piggy bank I was looking for, so Mr.

John gave me the direction to their other store. But that was way across

town, and unfortunately it was the rush hour traffic. Fortunately, as I

was driving out of that store parking lot, I saw a bus; it was

one of the public transportation buses in my beautiful city. I noticed an advertisement on that bus that read, "Ride Marta, It's Smarter." I was so

delighted to get another means of saving money because if I had to drive

across town, then I would end up burning too much gasoline (petrol) and

probably will not be on time for my next appointment, which was then

one and a half hours away. I always do have coins in my car so it would

not be a problem having enough to slot into the ticket machine. This

company upgraded their machines now so you can pay with your credit

or debit cards. Riding on that kind of public transportation is also good

for the environment too.

Just outside, on my way to the train station, I saw the man we just

had a conversation within that store at the bus stop, although he had left

in a hurry earlier, so I had assumed he was gone already. I asked him if

he needed a ride; and he yelled, "Yes, my man!"

I asked him, "Why are you still at the bus stop since you left almost

fifteen minutes ago?" Then he explained that the buses come around

every fifteen minutes, that he was in a hurry to get there on time but

unfortunately missed that bus. So, we finally introduced ourselves, although Mr. John told me a little about him earlier at the store. But I'd

"Equal rights and justice for all people"

78

rather not continue to dampen his soul with his unemployment situation,

I decided to be quiet. And since the train station was very close

by, I could avoid striking any conversation. Eric was quiet too in the

car, but I noticed he was carrying a laptop bag, a folder, and a water

bottle. He reached into his pocket and brought out a white handkerchief.

I thought he did not need that because it was springtime, and

that day was beautiful, not hot. But I noticed he was

sweating, also fidgeting, with that handkerchief. I was forced to break

that silence and asked him if he was okay.

It was as if he was waiting for me to utter a word; then he started

telling me about the horrible situation he had been in because of the

bad global economy, how he lost his job and the two cars they had in

his family. They lost one car by selling it to pay their rent and to buy

groceries when he was laid off and his wife just had a baby, so she

could not work either. Their other car was repossessed because all their

bills were over ninety days delinquent, and they could not get a loan

because of their bad credit.

Eric also mentioned that his wife decided to go back to school

to become a registered nurse but she was unable to secure a grant or scholarship. I felt so bad for him. We got to the train station. When he

was getting down, he got his laptop bag and the water bottle but forgot

to pick up his folder, so I called his attention to that. He smiled and said,

"Thank you! That contains my resumes and some other paperwork."

I was stunned for a second or two; from what Eric had just told

me about what he was going through, I knew it was bad but could not

believe some people had it that bad. One of the many reasons I asked

if we could exchange phone numbers was in case, I was in a position to

help him out in the event of any full-time job opportunity.

I had planned to ride the train too, but then I was contemplating if

I should just continue driving my car toward downtown or go and park,

as I had thought earlier to save money on gasoline (petrol) as one of

my austerity measures. Also, the time would be wasted in the rush hour

traffic: but I was getting lazy to go and park, then buy the train ticket. I

was feeling depressed at that moment because of what Eric just told me

about the hardship he and his family were going through.

I thought of starting to ride the train to fulfill my obligations whenever

I had engagements in downtown but thought I should start that another day.

"Equal rights and justice for all people"

79

Then I remembered I promised myself to do things as planned and to stop

procrastinating. I drove down to the next train station, and I was amazed

they had a big parking lot; I was so delighted because of my new discovery

that would save me money too by not paying for the parking space when I

get to the downtown. I went to park my car and got my train ticket.

I was waiting for the next train going south. Somebody yelled, "What's up?"

I looked back, and it happened to be Lawrence, one of my clients.

I noticed while he walks toward me, he was carrying a water bottle

and holding a handkerchief too. Then I had a thought process for a few

seconds. I wondered if that was a fashion statement or a way of life,

maybe it was something people had to do to adapt to the bad global

economy, so I asked myself how could carrying a water bottle and

holding a handkerchief be related to that?

We exchanged pleasantries, and I asked him where he had disappeared

to because the last time we saw each other was almost a year. And he

told me he went to Rome and Athens.

Wow! That should be a lot of fun, and jokingly I said, "At least some

people still have some money to go overseas on vacation." Then he

looked at me as if he had seen a ghost. I thought for a second why he

was giving me that kind of facial expression.

Then he said, "I had been out of job for almost a year and that was

one of the many reasons I had never bothered to call you or stop by your

office." He said he could not pay his bills especially the rent (house rent)

and his car note (monthly payment for the car), so he gave up and went

to stay with his cousin in Athens, Georgia (not the city in Greece). Then

later he moved to Rome, Georgia (another city in Georgia State, USA).

So, I apologized and did not want him to feel bad or that I came

across as if I was making fun of him by not being compassionate about

his situation. We talked some more, and I happened to look toward the

train tunnel, it was pitch dark.

Suddenly I saw these two bright lights coming toward us from that

tunnel. I said to Lawrence, "Here comes the train." I noticed everybody

getting ready in anticipation to board the train. Lawrence and I shook

hands, and we said "Good luck! See you!"

I made it there on time, got my piggy bank, and later met with my

last client for that day. Since then, I always advise my clients to meet

"Equal rights and justice for all people"

80

me halfway on the train route if they did not lay too much emphasis on

coming to my office. I wish they could extend that rail network to the

other part of our city.

Later that day, I met a potential client at a computer store, and

we exchanged business cards. Then I realized she was a lawyer; but

earlier during our conversation, I knew she had just moved down to my

beautiful city on an assignment. We were about to leave the store, but it

was so cloudy, windy, and about to rain. In case I could give her a ride

to her car because it was a huge parking lot, I asked Vanessa, "Where

did you park?" Fortunately, I had parked so close. But she said she was

not driving and had never driven a car before. She would be in her late

twenties or early thirties, so I was shocked to hear that.

Then I asked her why, with disbelief. She said she had never seen

the need to drive because the public transportation "up north" where she

came from were efficient and covered almost the entire state. I thought

we needed that here too.

Recently, I heard in the news that the governor of one of the States

"Up north" in the United States—if I am not mistaken, New Jersey—that they did not have enough money to finance a tunnel project from New

Jersey to New York. And there was a comment on the radio that the

federal government used to finance that kind of project like some

of the historic highways and bridges. But since the *"too* big to fail"

financial institutions got all the money, nothing was left to finance

important projects for the common people. The other rich companies or

deep-pocket companies are uncertain now of the outcome of

the global financial downturn, so they were holding tight to

their money and not helping to finance some important projects

as ever.

I don't blame them.

My other saving tip are for bookstores, e.g., Barnes & Noble and

BORDERS Books-Music-Café in my beautiful city. These bookstores

have *free* Wi-Fi Internet connection and clean restrooms

(toilets), but the

coffee is *not* free. So, from time to time, I just buy a small cup of coffee

or cake. I do not care much for coffee, but I feel compelled

to buy something at least in appreciation of the great environment they

created for the masses. Another venue is the public library, although

you do not need your own laptop (computer), but the Internet access is

limited and to be precise to like an hour.

"Equal rights and justice for all people"

81

I wish our local government can provide a place like the library or

upgrade the libraries that common people can go with their laptops and

have free Internet access, and others without their laptops could have

access to the Internet for at least two to three hours. I think

once the economy gets better, we should start creating businesses like

Internet cafés.

My other ways of saving money were getting free ice, and you can

put some air in your tires for free, at the QuikTrip (QT) gas station in

my neighborhood—great customer service with *clean* toilets. Most of

the time, I make sure I buy gasoline from them and many times never

compare if their gasoline was cheaper as ever, but for solidarity. You can

profit from great customer service.

My associate invited me to his son's football practice the other day

and said we could stop at the QT gas station to get a bag of free ice. I

looked at him with dismay but corrected him that it was a free cup or

couple of cups of free ice. But if he insisted on picking a free *bag* of ice,

then I would rather wait for him in the car; in case he got arrested for shoplifting, then I would be in the better position to call his wife to go

and bail him out.

We continued to talk politics. He lamented over and over on how

frustrating it could be without a job or any source of income. *He thinks*

women should take over running the government. But he smiled and

said he was just being sarcastic.

No! I told him it was a matter of fact that women should take over,

but he shook his head in disapproval and said, "Not in our lifetime."

Then I asked him again, "So you don't think women should take over and run things?"

He did not utter a word. His eyes were wandering around for a

second or two as if what I just asked was a rhetorical question or to

him probably not substantial or worth laying too much emphasis on

because from our conversation earlier, I realized he concluded it was

not practical to see women in that role as presidents, especially

in the developed countries. Anyway, I replied that all I asked was to

start creating the awareness for all to see the reasons why women

should be running our government worldwide, especially in the

developed countries.

Fortunately, we are in the computer era with the latest innovations

in electronics, wireless communication technology is getting

"Equal rights and justice for all people"

82

better and still evolving. Most of us use this means of communication,

and the number is growing at an exponential rate. We all just witnessed

the presidential election in one of the most developed and democratic

countries in the world. Most of us never thought this would come to

pass. It was beyond our wildest imagination.

One of the things that aided that presidential election was the

power of the Internet; we can use this communication medium too to

create the awareness as per electing women as our presidents. They

have the natural ability and the skills set to nurture our countries

worldwide.

"The central problem of our age is how to act decisively in the absence

of certainty".

—Bertrand Russell

It had been a while since I visited my favorite store, and I

had to see Mr. John because I knew he could help to analyze some of the

things I noticed in our society. I was still puzzled about seeing people

carrying water bottles and holding handkerchiefs. I got to Mr. John's

store, but it was so busy probably because of the holiday weekend; also

because that was a real bargain store, so I thought that would not be a good time to have a chitchat with him.

I walked around few aisles. I could not find him, so I thought he was

probably off that day. Although I met Mr. John once, I could recognize

him so easily because of the manner he placed his glasses on the tip of

his nose and bowed his head slightly when he looked at people as if he

was spying. I decided to leave and hoped I would be lucky to see him

next time I stopped by.

I was just about to exit the store, and I heard somebody say, "How

are you doing, young man?" I looked back because that voice sounded

so familiar. It was Mr. John. Then we exchanged pleasantries, and I

asked how his wife, Ms. Ruth, was doing.

She was on vacation visiting their daughter in California that just

had a baby. I congratulated him and asked why he did not go with her.

He said he had already used up his vacation time, but he planned to go

during the Christmas holiday because their store will be closed, and he

had some sick leave days to add to that. He pulled out his wallet, then

said, "Let me show you my children and grandchildren."

"Equal rights and justice for all people"

83

I was still viewing the pictures and said, "These are beautiful pictures."

Before I could pass any other comment, Mr. John said, "My wife is Korean." Apparently, I could see that. He met her in Korea when he was serving his country. Mr. John had two children in their mid-thirties. The man was in the military as an engineer, and his daughter, Catherine, that his wife was visiting, was a registered nurse. In fact, Mr. John had a beautiful family.

Then I told him that it was so busy in their store that day because I could see long lines up front by the cashiers. Mr. John said, "I am on my lunch break now."

I was glad to know that so we could talk some more; then I could ask him some questions. So, I asked him if he was going out for lunch, but he replied he had his lunch at their break room already but still had another fifteen minutes before his break would be over. He asked if I was in a hurry. I told him that I intentionally stopped over at his store to see if we could talk because I had some questions for him.

Then we decided to walk out of the store. I had parked my car far away, but Mr. John suggested we could go and sit down to talk in his

truck since he parked closer. We were approaching a red truck, so I

asked him, "Is that your truck?"

Mr. John smiled and said, "That's my baby." In fact, that was a

beautiful, well-kept antique truck. He said he bought it new and that he

was the only owner for the past thirty-two years. He had just spent over

six thousand dollars to refurbish both the interior and the exterior.

That truck looked so clean both in and out, I was so impressed.

Mr. John's truck reminded me of the truck in an old TV comedy series,

Sanford & Son. I told Mr. John I finally got my piggy bank, a big one.

Then he smiled and gave me a thumb-up as if I had just won a money

lottery and said, "Way to go, young man." I found his acknowledgment

and remark somewhat overrated because I just got a piggy bank, but

I think it was a way to start saving money without realizing it. So, his

positive reaction because I finally got the piggy bank was a good one.

Mr. John would be in his early or mid-sixties, had good well-to-do

children that can support him, and he was getting his retirement salary from the military. So, I was wondering why he was still going through

"Equal rights and justice for all people"

84

that headache of working at that store. I was just about to ask him, but

before I could utter a word, it was as if he could read my mind.

He said, "Yes! I could have retired two years ago, but I love to work."

And they want to buy their retirement home in Florida *without* financing

it. Then he said, "I will be retiring in six months and going fishing." He

pulled out his wallet again and showed me the home they were about to

purchase.

Then I asked him about what I have been noticing in our society,

why most people were carrying water bottles and handkerchiefs.

Mr. John said, "Look here! Look here! Look here, young man! That

is one of the symptoms of economic hardship syndrome (EHS)."

I knew when Mr. John continued to say, "Look here!" before making

most of his point, that was going to be fun conversation because that was

his way of getting people's attention. I was ready for that too, but for

a few seconds, I wished I had never asked him about that observation

because I did not want to get into any abstract conversation with Mr.

John nor Tony or encourage him to start arguments on why he thinks the

world was coming to an end.

So I told him I listen to the news, and WebMD was one of my

favorite websites, so I was knowledgeable and current on health care

issues. Where did he get the term "EHS"?

He argued I would not get that from any news or the WebMD, that no

medical doctor can cure EHS but only our political leaders worldwide,

once they do the right thing to eradicate the sufferings of the common

people. Surprisingly, nowadays EHS was not only a common people's

disease, Mr. John continued, but also affecting the rich and the affluent

because they know they will eventually be making less money because

they are eliminating the middle class by not creating skilled jobs or jobs

in general. Eventually in this kind of scenario, the security of the rich

and the affluent people in our societies worldwide is in jeopardy too. So

I asked Mr. John for the symptoms of EHS:

Ö Trying as much as possible not to make eye contact with others

because you think they will see you are in financial problem.

And always looking around everywhere you go to see if there is

free money lying at a corner for you to pick up. Unfortunately

you might not find that because most people are holding on tight

to the little money they have now.

"Equal rights and justice for all people"

85

Ö After pumping gasoline (petrol) at the station, raising and jiggling the gasoline hose to make sure you get the last drop of your gasoline.

Ö Becoming antisocial, moody, and easily irritated.

Ö Always carrying your water bottle filled with your tap water from
home or wherever you can get free water to avoid buying one. And that the handkerchief is for wiping off your sweat. Sweating on a cold day (wintertime) is because you are actually sweating from within, and that could be due to high blood pressure.

Ö Easily irritated, unnecessary aggressiveness, rudeness, increase in domestic abuse, increase in crime rate.

Ö Getting to the gasoline station and contemplating on how much
you should spend on gasoline. Tried your credit card, and it was denied because you have no money left on it. You then decided to
check the glove box in your car for loose change, and hopefully it's up to two dollars because most of us do not feel comfortable buying gasoline at less than that.

Ö Doing whatever it takes to keep your job: working thirty to forty-five minutes extra with no pay (pay attention: rush hour starts 5:30 p.m. nowadays instead of 4:45 p.m.). Some people will offer to help the boss clean up his or her yard on weekends and also offering to baby-sit for free.

Ö More people getting involved in scams (fraudulent practices) all
over the world in addition to the main inventors of scams.

Ö No more real smiles but plastic smiles

Ö More people going online for illness diagnosis, so they can buy drugs over the counter instead of visiting the medical doctors because of no medical insurance.

Ö So many people losing weight because of starvation and some gaining excessive weight because of bad diet.

Ö Worn-out shoes due to excessive job searches without positive result, so no money to buy new shoes.

I told Mr. John few of these symptoms were kind of similar to depression.

He agreed, but the major difference was that no medical doctor can cure

EHS, and the World Health Organization (WHO) doesn't know about this

acronym. Only our political leaders worldwide have the cure for EHS.

I eventually asked Mr. John for his phone number. I gave him mine

and promised him once Ms. Ruth gets back from California, they would

"Equal rights and justice for all people"

86

be invited for dinner at my place. I told him unfortunately I could not

cook, but I would order any food of their choice.

He said, "That's a plan, young man." Then we shook hands and said

good-bye. But I know Mr. John's EHS talk was a joke.

I went to visit Tony, my lawyer friend, and brought up the conversation

about the world coming to an end; and Tony's input on these assumptions

was kind of abstract just as Mr. John's. Tony's stand on what he thinks

about aliens: he believes they are real, that they are in those

other planets, and that they check on us from time to time with probably

the intention to invade planet Earth. That's why we have the unidentified

flying objects (UFOs).

Tony was serious about his assumptions. I guessed probably

because he was a *Star Trek* junkie. Nobody in their right mind would

believe that. I could not say he was not smart because we all think most

lawyers are intelligent, and they could make us believe the color

purple is red. But I was not buying into Tony's analogy because he also

mentioned the asteroids were stones thrown from the other planets by

some invisible inhabitants (aliens) in that planet, that they had actually thrown a big asteroid that would take years to fall and smash planet

Earth.

Wow! I wondered if Tony really believed what he was telling me or

probably just hallucinating. I assumed Tony was going through another

phase in life and could not differentiate fiction from non-fiction. He also

suggested we human beings should attack them first because

fortunately, we are aggressive, and offense is always the best form of

defense. With all our new technology, our nuclear bomb and advanced

air force arsenals, we must invade those aliens as soon as possible once

our global economy gets better. Then we could research and develop the

technology to find them.

Tony was so serious that we must be *man* enough and act fast. And

jokingly, I told him that once we invaded them, destroy all of them and

their other planet, we must bring all their electric cars to Earth, to all the

people that had their cars repossessed because they lost their jobs due

to the global economy disaster partially due to bad management by our

leaders. Then our political leaders worldwide could promise them free

cars as one of their main projects for the common people.

"Equal rights and justice for all people"

87

I also suggested to Tony that we could also take over their planet.

then the rich and the affluent people could move there because they can

afford it. I guessed Tony came back to his senses and told me he was

sure, their planet might not be life-sustainable for human beings, and he

yelled at me, "Can't you see they never wear clothes? These are strange

people!" Unattractive species.

"Beauty in things exists in the mind which contemplates them."

—David Hume (1711-1776)

Although I did not believe aliens are real as Tony's illusion,

emphasizing they were real but assuming there are aliens somewhere

in the outer space, I bet their new world would be so boring because

of these aliens' attributes: they all looked alike; talked alike (actually

they talked funny); they did not have the right physique for most sports

especially football, hockey, or basketball; and they never wear clothes,

no fashion trends.

On second thought, maybe their new world will be better because

of just one main language. That means better understanding when they

communicate. They all look alike—that means less distraction; they refer to each other as my people and that could promote better harmony

among those aliens. But I think their new world will be boring without

sports like football and basketball.

And they look too serious. I bet their politicians will not be

posting negative advertisements. Most of us knew those negative

advertisements were ridiculous and outrageous, but when the economy

was good, most of enjoyed them because they were funny and nothing

substantial. Most of those negative advertisements were

baseless; but on second thought, those negative advertisements and

some rhetoric by our political leaders could incite violence.

To be realistic, there are some political extremists out there, and

some of the things (rhetoric) that most of us take lightly or find funny

might be taken seriously by some political extremists. You never know

how this group of people (political extremists) would react; some of

them could even take that as far as becoming foot soldiers.

So, it will be better for our politicians to reduce negative advertisements

because the common people are not finding them funny. Maybe your

"Equal rights and justice for all people"

"

88

peers find them interesting, but the common people are suffering, so

at this moment we are not really being entertained by your negative

advertisements. So, to our political leaders worldwide, please promise

things (agendas and issues) only when you know you can do what you

promised, putting the bipartisan efforts and support into consideration

too. Do not just promise anything that would get you elected.

I said adios to Tony, and we planned to meet later the next Friday.

"Equal rights and justice for all people"

89

Women's natural nurturing Abilities and Great Values

I

stopped over at Tony's house later that Friday as promised. Tony and
I had a way of greeting one another like every other people do when
you meet a friend. Tony normally says, "Bonjour, monsieur," and my
response is always *"Que pasa, amigo"* in Spanish and never a direct
response to Tony's greetings in French. I noticed recently and wondered
why Tony always liked to insert a word or two of French from time to
time during conversations.
So, I asked, "Are you learning how to speak French now or preparing
to communicate better in French when you go and visit your children in
Paris?" He responded that he had French-speaking people in his
bloodline and told me how his ancestors migrated from Morocco (North
Africa) in the early 1800s to France, and in 1865 some of them moved
to England. His great-grandfather later migrated to the United States in
early 1905. Then I asked him how he knew all that.
He smiled and said he had something to show me. He invited me

to his basement, then I followed him downstairs. I was curious to see

what he wanted to show me but hoped it was not one of those abstract

things because Tony had the habit of bringing up abstract topics, and

most of the time, I found it difficult to see any logic in most of those

conversations.

So, I followed him, and we were on our way to his basement. I had known

Tony for almost ten years but visited their basement just once—although

he did not open the couple of the doors in that basement my first time

down there. I had never asked him where those doors led to.

"Equal rights and justice for all people"

90

I was still wondering what might be new. Tony paused when he got

in front of one of those doors I had just mentioned. He looked at me

and said, "You are one of the few people I will ever allow into this room

because you are not just a friend, but you are already part of my family."

Okay, I felt honored but could not wait for him to open that door fast

enough.

We got into that room. That room gave me the sensation as if I was

back to the past. All the furniture were antique. In one side of the room,

there were three bookshelves arranged side by side. The one in the

middle was almost to the ceiling of that room, that bookshelf

had a beautiful antique clock with a pendulum. I was so impressed but

still wondering why Tony treated that room as sacred.

My eyes were wandering all over that room. I noticed there was

an antique telescope at a corner. I moved closer to see it and noticed it

was truly antique but had most of the features of the modern telescope.

Tony and I enjoyed viewing the stars. Then I asked Tony that he knew I

was saving to buy a telescope and why he had never mentioned he had another one at the basement. At least he could have suggested I buy the

one in his office upstairs; then he could use that one at the basement.

But he replied, "I never had the intention of using that telescope.

It is something I see as an antique decoration to admire." I understood

where he was coming from because I had some antique decorations too

but not as expensive as Tony's. I noticed some books on the shelves but

they all looked alike. I moved closer and realized they were a series of

old law books: they were kind of like the ones in his home office upstairs.

In another bookshelf, one of the books caught my attention. It was

a red book, so it stood out. I asked Tony if I could look at that.

It was among the philosophy books, and the title read *Marriage Is a*

Sacred Union, with the subtitle, *The Woman and the Man Become One.*

I opened it, read few lines, and flipped through the six-hundred-page

book in about sixty seconds.

Tony said, "My mother gave me that book thirty-two years ago when

I was age seven." She taught him family values, and his father was a

disciplinarian.

Tony said that his mom was originally from Spain, that her family moved to the United States in 1945, and that I reminded him of his mom

"Equal rights and justice for all people"

91

whenever I said, "*Que pasa, amigo.*" She was not fluent in speaking

English: but his dad was fluent in French, English, and Spanish.

"I wish I could speak so many languages like your dad," I replied.

Speaking Spanish fluently could help me build more clientele. I bought

a software program to learn how to speak some other languages, and it

contained over fifty languages, but I had been procrastinating to start

for almost three years. The package was still intact since it was

delivered. So, I said, "What do you want to show me?"

I could see him slide one of the paintings on the wall to the side but

seemed he was having some problems with the code to open a safe box

hidden behind that painting. Then he had to call his wife, Camilia, to get

the code. Finally, he got that safe box opened and brought out a black

folder with some black stripes.

I glanced at the imprint on that folder, and it read, "Back to the Past,

Inc." Their mission statement read, "We will take you back as far as Adam

and Eve." Initially, I thought that was a joke. But when I read through

how that company analyzed their findings and conclusions, and they

also applied methods using the blood type, genealogy, history of family, by step-by-step analyses of the line of descent from their ancestors, and

the DNA, I was so impressed.

Tony told me the price, but I thought that was expensive. But it could

be fun when you have the money to invest on knowing your family tree

with charts and tables that show the line of descendants from an ancestor.

Tony mentioned he stopped the project since 2007 when the economy

started going sour. You must impose some austerity measures and

watch the way you spend, focus on things that are important in the order

of preference.

I noticed in Tony's family tree that at a particular time, they were

common people, then a royal family. Surprisingly they were grouped as

slaves in another period of time, and a later period as common people.

So, I wondered why their status continued to change from one period to

another. My only assumption was since there was no democratic system

in all those regions in those days, a king could just wake up one day,

decide to wage war on another region, and when he won, he would then

take everybody in that region that were still alive as slaves. I also read it was normal then for kings to have as many wives as possible. Actually

some of the women slaves became the king's wives or concubines because

I read in Tony's family tree that one of his ancestors was a queen, and

"Equal rights and justice for all people"

92

she was later a slave. But some of the descendants from her after the

period that she was grouped as a slave were grouped as royal families.

That means she later married a king or was one of the king's concubines

at that period.

Just before I left Tony's place, I congratulated him for winning his

case. It was about domestic abuse, and there had been a rise in domestic

abuse cases again because of the bad economy. The wife (plaintiff)

sued the husband (defendant) because he was always physically and

emotionally abusing her and the children. The husband happened to be

the breadwinner in that family. Unfortunately, he lost his full-time job

too.

He (the husband) was told he could get a well-paying part-time job

by working at the site of the recent oil spill for $25 an hour. He got there

and was then frustrated about the failed promise of that job prospect. He

eventually started drinking and drug abuse, so it resulted in violating his

family.

Although he got letters of good behavior from his former co-workers, former employers, and friends to prove he was a good man, that did not

help because the medical report the wife presented at the courthouse

was enough to find him guilty as charged for domestic abuse. So, the bad

global economy was not only affecting our financial situation but could

also result into negative ways of life like domestic abuse.

"Equal rights and justice for all people"

93

Gender equality

ony asked if I had some time so we could stop over at Dr. Henry's

office. Dr. Henry was Tony's family doctor; I had met him couple of

times before, a very nice guy but kind of opinionated on most issues,

especially sports and politics. I enjoyed having conversations with him

in general, but he thought his basketball team will beat the other teams

to a pulp that season because his basketball team had the best of the best

in men's professional basketball teams.

We got to his office, and Tony picked up his yearly physical report.

Come to think of it, I should be going for my physical checkup yearly

too. Apart from the peace of mind health wise, it is also good for the

insurance companies so they don't have to come up with a big lump

sum of money in case I come down with a complicated health problem

because of my being irresponsible. Going for the yearly physical

checkup could reduce my health premium and reduce the money

the government spends on subsidizing the health insurance.

We were just on our way out of Dr. Henry's office, then he brought

up the conversation on the performance of his favorite team, Miami Heat (a professional basketball team in the United States). I sighed because I

knew once he got started on that, we would be there for another twenty

to thirty minutes, although I was in a hurry, I always enjoyed that kind

of conversation too.

Because initially, during that season, I thought all the

other teams were doomed because I assumed Dr. Henry's favorite team

(Miami Heat) would be too hot to handle for my team—actually, my

teams, because I have two favorite teams. One of my teams actually

had the best performance in the previous year, and my other team was

"Equal rights and justice for all people"

T

94

my home team, although they seldom perform well. But I believe in

solidarity, especially for my beautiful home state. Also, most of us cheer

for the underdogs to see if they could just pull themselves out of the hole

and surprise all. Some other underdogs were not worth cheering

for, so it will be wishful thinking if you expect them to; they might not

even qualify (substandard) to be in that competition or league

to start with. But my home team could compete but just needed some

more jigsaw cards to complete the puzzle.

For instance, I was really frustrated when LeBron James (one of the

best professional basketball players in this millennium) and his team had

a series with my home team last year. As much as I loved his performance

as a basketball player, I was disappointed when he repeatedly dunked on

my home team. We all knew they were going to beat us, but I thought

that kind of display of superiority was an overkill and uncalled-for. I

knew it was just a game, but most of us get so emotional about sports.

But as for me, I never carry that emotion for more than thirty minutes

after the game. It was just a game, so enjoy it!

While we were still talking, the phone rang, and that was Dr. Henry's

wife on the phone. Dr. Henry picked up the phone and yelled, "Hello,

Mama Michelly!" That was the day I found out Mama Michelly

was Dr. Henry's wife; I used to think he was talking to his mother. Then

Dr. Henry, during their conversation, asked the wife to hold on and then

asked us if we would love to join them for dinner next Saturday at 6:00

p.m.? Tony and I looked at one another and nodded our heads in approval

to join Dr. and Mrs. Henry for dinner.

I picked up Tony in my fuel-economical car. I would have loved to

have a hybrid car like Tony's, but they were kind of expensive when they

first got to the market. Just like any electronic gadget, they are always

expensive when newly introduced to the market I would have

preferred an all-electric car, but I bet it would be farfetched at that

moment. Also, I read they still must improve the interior comfort and

the battery cells to get more mileage per charge. We got to Dr.

Henry's neighborhood and called him from the call box to let us in.

In fact, that was a beautiful, big, and gated subdivision, the scenery

of the landscape and the well-manicured lawns. I saw some people jogging and some walking their dogs. We parked on their private driveway,

walked to the door and rang their doorbell. Dr. Henry answered the door

"Equal rights and justice for all people"

95

to welcome us in. Their kitchen was slightly to the right, and I saw a lady

in the kitchen, but she was petite with a baby face. She looked so young,

and I thought that was the daughter.

Then Dr. Henry introduced her to me, "Meet my beautiful wife, Michelle," and introduced me to her too; then we shook hands in turns.

She knew Tony already.

She was so excited to tell us that we were going to try her new recipe

and hoped we enjoyed it. She went back into the kitchen; in less than

ten minutes, there was a sweet aroma coming from Mrs. Henry's kitchen

that filled up the whole living room with a delicious smell.

Then I complimented her that the food smelled delicious already.

She replied, "You just wait until you taste this."

I yelled, "Can't wait." She came out of the kitchen and suggested I

should have a copy of the recipe. She probably assumed I was married

or loved to cook, unfortunately neither at that moment. To avoid the long

story why I was not married or not really interested in cooking, I agreed

to have a copy of that recipe, and she was so pleased. She rushed to their

computer room to print me a copy.

The way I was brought up, apart from being the last born and the only boy in my immediate family, to my understanding then, the women

were supposed to cook, then the housemaid does the cleaning and the

dishes. That was a bad orientation. I was surprised that grown men do

laundry, especially dishes, in most of the developed countries. I used to

think a man's only responsibility was to make money, to take care of his

family, and of course, protect them too.

Michelle called Andy from the kitchen (I knew she was referring to

the husband because Tony calls Dr. Henry as Andy sometimes). Then

she stepped out briefly and told us how Dr. Henry was never interested

in cooking and would not even help with the house cleaning; it was

as if she could read my mind. I was still going through the guilt trip

of not being responsible, for not helping the women with the cleaning,

cooking, and doing laundry.

Then Dr. Henry murmured to us in a very low voice in response to

her remarks, "I am the only one wearing the pants in this family." And

boys will be boys, as we all say, so we both acknowledged his stand

on that issue by nodding in approval. But sincerely, we were just being barbaric; it would be better to wake up, adapt to the new millennium,

and stop seeing our women as modern slaves.

"Equal rights and justice for all people"

96

Tony, Dr. Henry, and I continued our conversation while Mrs. Henry

was still busy preparing our dinner. And for a second, to the left side

of where I was sitting, I saw a dog running down the stairs; I

thought that dog was going to attack me. I stayed calm because I learned

that you should show that you are not scared in that kind of situation or

else the animal might attack you. And again, I am a man— "men must

never show any sign of weakness."

While I was still going on that thought, Dr. Henry noticed that dog

too and called her "*Boobee*" and told me she was a beautiful and friendly

dog but always excited when she sees strangers. She just wanted to play.

and Dr. Henry said, "Sit down" to that dog, introduced her as "Boobee,"

and said that she was just a big puppy. I was impressed with the manner

Boobee responded to Dr. Henry's command. She sat there quietly but

after some time started groaning again. Probably she was tired of sitting

and was in distress.

Dr. Henry noticed that too and told her to go and play with

her toys. Since Tony was familiar with this family, he brought up the conversation about their other pet, Tiger. So, he said, "So what happened

to Tiger?"

Where was Tiger? I thought these people used

to have a real tiger as a pet. Tony noticed the look at me and said

Tiger was Andy's (Dr. Henry's) male dog, but that dog had a

mind of his own. He was so aggressive, obnoxious despite being trained

at a top-of-the-line dog training school as Boobee. I said, "Anyway, boys

must be boys."

Andy said his cousin was in their place on vacation, and he and Tiger

became attached, so he gave Tiger to his cousin. He had started barking

almost every night and became a nuisance in their neighborhood. Then

I told him that he could have bought one of the new products that could

make a dog to stop barking.

Andy said, "Probably, but that might be too late," and again said that

he had enough of Tiger.

We continued our conversation, and Mrs. Henry probably overheard

some of our conversation. She peeped out of the kitchen and said, "You

men . . ." Later when she was serving us dinner, she said, "You men are

generally narcissistic."

Then she continued by saying, "I think your executive functioning is four, on the scale of one to ten," and that was one of the many reasons we

"Equal rights and justice for all people"

97

are continuously losing the ability to rule and make tangible decisions.

She continued by saying, "Don't you guys think it's about time to give

women the chance to take a shot at it, and maybe things could start

working right again?" None of us responded to that question because we

took that as a rhetorical question.

Then she suddenly changed the topic and started talking about some

new flowers she was going to plant in front of their house during the

springtime. Tony and I gave Mrs. Henry lots of compliments for that

delicious dinner: we did really enjoy their company. And we shook

hands, and Andy escorted us to the door.

Tony and I did enjoy their company and her food. She was also sweet

and accommodating. Tony acknowledged that and said, "Yes! They

were, and those were one of the best couples ever." He told me that they

related like brother and sister. You wish to get married

when you experience such a togetherness.

But I was still mesmerized with Mrs. Henry's input on men and

politics because most of the time, while we were there, she did not say

much. I understood men being narcissistic, but the executive functioning phrase was new to me; I thought my use of the English grammar should

be at least seven on a scale of one to ten.

I decided to ask Tony since he was a lawyer, so I assumed he might

be familiar with some English words that were not readily available in the

dictionary. I came to find out executive functioning was psychological

term, and Tony also said Mrs. Henry throws around some psychology jargon

during conversations, that she had a doctorate degree in clinical psychology

and had her own private practice. I was shocked to know that she had

all that education and made as much or better than her husband.

Tony said Dr. Henry nicknamed his wife "Mama Michelly" because

he said she was a friend and like a mother figure when they were in

college. Mrs. Michelle Henry was actually a year senior to Dr. Henry in

college. It was like a bulb lighted up in my brain; then I realized that we

men always assume women are inferior.

And I recollected when Dr. Henry said, "I am the only one wearing

the pants in this house." I wondered where that thought was coming

from, for him to make such a comment—man's ego? I know from the beginning of time, we like to believe men must always be in charge, but

that was then. Things are really changing, and we must learn to adapt to

this new age.

"Equal rights and justice for all people"

98

It's about time for equal opportunity for all. I listen to the National

Public Radio (NPR) in the United States from time to time especially

when I am driving, and you can listen to their podcast too anywhere in

the world via the Internet. I would love to recommend this radio

station for all, especially in the United States. Most of the NPR programs

are educational. You can get lots of important information from this radio

station that could benefit you and others immensely. I want to seize this

opportunity to tell you to help fund their programs; they have fund drives

from time to time, but it is a shame that I never sent them any money

during these fund drives but promise to do that as soon as possible.

On NPR I was fortunate to listen to Teri Gross, one of the best

interviewers. You have to listen to her interviews and experience her style

of interviewing. It is as if she stammers a little bit in the beginning of

every sentence as if as she is giving the interviewee the chance to get his

or her thoughts together, and most of her questions are brilliant. So Teri

Gross was interviewing a bestseller author the other day; he was recently on the cover of *TIME* magazine for the extraordinary accomplishment

of his latest book. I think his book was telling the story about

a particular woman, although I did not get the chance to listen to the

entire interview. But if I was not mistaken, she (the character in that

book) went against all odds, ignoring the stigma of what a woman was

supposed to do or not, to build her family in a new married life.

Most female authors were not really pleased for the extraordinary

recognition of this male author although he was once a bestseller author.

But the women felt that was another slap on the face because female

authors have written something similar previously and none of them

were honored by putting their picture on the cover of a well-known

newsmagazine such as *TIME*. They perceived that as one of the many

double standards in the men's world.

I was biased at the beginning of that interview and also perceived

that as one of the many injustices against the female gender. But after

listening to the response of that author being interviewed—apart from

being a brilliant author, he had a good sense of humor too—I did

understand his point of view. I realized from his response that it was not as if he lobbied to be on the cover page of *TIME* magazine; but as we all

know, many times men are always in charge, and they make most of the

decisions in most of the companies or establishments.

"Equal rights and justice for all people"

99

My friend argued with me once because I was comparing *The
Oprah Winfrey Show* (Oprah is one of the greatest interviewers
and the

best in that business) to the *Larry King Live* show (one of the
greatest

interviewers too). And let's not forget one of the pioneers of that
type of

forum, Barbara Walters.

So, my argument was that they are all on top of their game and
their

shows educate, benefit, and influence lots of their audience.
Actually

most of us will miss these shows when they eventually go
permanently

off the airwaves. My point was not that I preferred *women* radio
or TV

personnel with high rating. I like Neal Bootz, the talk show host
on WSB radio, and I was crucified for saying his show was
educational

and funny to me. I liked him although I did not agree with some
of his

ideologies.

My point was that we have women in different fields and
specialties

that are equal and sometimes better than their men associate, but
we

never give them their deserving recognition. That's all I ask for
and to

start creating the awareness.

If there is equality between men and women, we do not really
need

advocates for women's rights. Sometimes, it feels as if we treat women

as subhuman, second-class, and not equal to us in numerous ways, also

in the manner we relate to them. You rarely hear the term "advocate for

men's rights" because many times we are the "oppressors." Normally

the oppressors (men) do not need an advocate, but the "oppressed"

(women) do. We can all notice whenever there was a war or natural

disaster anywhere in the world, women carry most of the burdens of

the aftermath of these unfortunate incidents, and most of them will

be forced into prostitution or other abuses by men to survive. A good

example of these kinds of ugly situations is still going on in Haiti after

the recent earthquake.

As men we are always in the positions of authority, so we make most

of the decisions. We must be more compassionate and do more to

eradicate the sufferings of women and children worldwide.

"The true republic: men, their rights and nothing more; women, their

rights and nothing less."

—Susan B. Anthony (1820-1906)

"Equal rights and justice for all people"

100

One of the many scenarios we all witness all the time and might take

forever to change, if ever. A good example is in sports, like the Women's

National Basketball Association (WNBA) games in North America. I

like basketball, but if it's not the NBA games, which are all-men, I was

not excited.

I happened to see one of the WNBA games accidentally while playing

around with my remote control, then I was just curious to see if there

would be any action, but to my dismay, these women were very good too

but not as physical as most of the NBA games. I say most NBA

games, but an NBA game doesn't have to be physical before I

enjoy it. If you are an NBA fan, the L.A. Lakers are not that physical.

and at the same time, one of the best, the Arizona Suns for example, are

not always physical but play with finesse. At the same time, we find their

games interesting, and they are top performers in the NBA.

So, for us men not to promote or sponsor women's games in general

because we are always in charge of most decision-making positions is all

basically, of our egotistic, chauvinistic, and superiority complex. As men with our "see me, I am on top and in charge" attitude, maybe we could

rethink and give the women the opportunity to perform or be in position

to perform too—I suggest, as a president. Trust me, we might all be

shocked to see women perform better. Although I mentioned earlier that

men are always in charge of most things, so we can assume we make

most of the decisions. But I'm always happy to see women's centers in

most of the hospitals or women's clinics in the developed countries. I

hope that kind of establishments are not just one of our selfish intentions

to create such great access and special care for women and hopefully not

just seeing them as baby machines to maintain the existence of human

beings.

The nurturing attribute is part of a woman's makeup, and the manner

she could apply this quality to nurture a family and also a nation—it's

about time. Imagine you are in a team, you are appointed to do a task,

and you are not really accomplishing much. I think is better to let other

members of your team take a shot at it. So, let's see women as our team members that are willing to participate in this project known as world

order (good living, peace, and better economy). This is not about

conservatism, liberalism, or being independent, *but* fairness to all, both

females and males.

"Equal rights and justice for all people"

101

I might be wrong, but I believe because we men are the one applying

all these ideologies, maybe we are not really doing a good job. Let the

women rule, especially in developed countries like the United States,

Germany, Canada, Russia, Great Britain, France, Japan, and others. I

prefer to see this happen in the above-mentioned countries because they

are on top of the world now. So, a woman becoming a president

in one of these countries through a democratic process. Then we see her

performance in two terms; at least then we would all see what we have

been missing. Somebody argued women turned things upside down from

the beginning of time as far back as Adam and Eve, but that argument

did not justify why we should prevent them from being in control of

things, especially electing them as presidents in our societies.

"If the first woman God ever made was strong enough to turn the world

upside down all alone, these women together ought to be able to turn it

back, and get it right side up again! And now they are asking to do it,

the men better let them".

—Sojourner Truth (1797-1883)

"Equal rights and justice for all people"

102

Perform Your Civic Rights

for a better society

ony scolded me the other day about not performing one of the main

civic rights, to go and vote during election time. He did not think I

had to travel to my hometown to accomplish that; I could just have

inquired if my country allowed voting abroad, then gone to the embassy

or consulate and cast my vote.

He said, "Your I—don't-care attitude about casting votes is not doing

you and that society any good," that I should stop complaining when things

are not going right for that country or some issues I believed in were not

implemented. **"You *must* vote, and it should be based on your conscience.**

That's one of the beauties of democracy . . . you have the power, so why

not use it and stop sitting on the fence?" Tony and I had arguments about

politics and my stand on some agendas and issues, and he tried to group

me as an *undecided voter.* But I do not like to be tagged as "undecided

voter" because it sounds like the "confused" group of people. I would

rather be an independent, not necessarily affiliated with any political party, but sometimes "independent" sounds like a loner and somebody that does

not believe in teamwork. So maybe a moderate in case I am interested

being part of one of the political parties; that would put me in the position

to analyze issues because I will be well-informed. Then I can vote on

substantial issues of interest and better choice of leaders to represent me.

The phone rang, and that was Tony's wife, Camilia, calling to

confirm her arrival time. She was coming back from Paris after visiting

their children in the boarding school.

Camilia sent Tony on some errands. Then we decided to go their

dry cleaner and the post office. Tony said we were going to ride this

"Equal rights and justice for all people"

T

103

time in their hybrid car because their top-of-the-line SUV was not

fuel economical. I smiled. I understood, and that was why I bought a

fuel-economical car. Although to be sincere, I prefer the interior comfort

of that SUV; but Tony was right, if we could all sacrifice some of these

luxuries, then our people will stop depending on foreign oil.

We were driving through some neighborhood, and Tony said, "Did

you see all those yard signs?"

And jokingly I replied, "Yes! The election yard sign about electing a

judge that read, 'He has been on the bench for thirty years.' Shouldn't he

be tired of sitting on the same bench for thirty years?"

Tony looked at me as if I was crazy and said they just used that phrase to show that judge's qualification.

Then I yelled at Tony, "I know that, and where is your sense of humor?"

He replied that actually previously, when he had mentioned the yard signs, he was referring to the "foreclosure" yard signs all over the

neighborhood. Sincerely I saw those too, but to keep my sanity, I always

tried to ignore them. The global economy was really bad, and the real

estate was feeling the impact in a big way.

Tony just got a text from Maddy if he was interested in an investment

property because she had just found a special deal. A particular property
was $145,000 last week, and now the price was greatly reduced to
$65,000. Wow! That was a steal, but Tony said he was not interested
because he felt he should hold on to what he had at that moment
because the way things were, it started getting scary to invest with the
little you had because the economic turnaround might take longer than
we thought. So it would be a risky business to start gambling with your
life savings.
I told him that he was even fortunate talking about his life savings,
that most people were living on paycheck to paycheck, and some had
nothing to live on. To become homeless nowadays is just a paycheck
away. Unfortunately, things were taking forever to get better, but to be on
the positive side, we can say "slow economy recovery" so we should just
"hold on tight" in anticipation that the economy will get better soon.
Do you know in Brazil, it is mandatory to vote during major elections
even if you are in another country? You must go to their (Brazilian)
embassy to vote. I just learned that once they are sixteen years old, they

"*Equal rights and justice for all people*"

104

are qualified to vote in Brazil. Brazil's economy is relatively

growing despite the global economic downturn.

I heard on the radio the other day, the interviewer was congratulating

one of the Brazilian political leaders and questioned him about the

progress of their economy. He replied, "We will continue to swim means

progressing, though some countries prefer to fly like an eagle." I think

that statement was so impressive. I wish in the near future, some of the

underdeveloped countries will continue to walk instead of this standstill

state, which is not good for their societies in general. Hopefully these

countries (Third World countries) will start learning baby steps to start

walking.

"Cast your vote. It's your right."

As I mentioned earlier in this book, I imposed some austerity
measures on myself, so I can cut my coat according to my size.
For
instance, another way to pass the time is by listening to the radio.
Somebody asked me why not watch television instead. But I told
her
most of my favorite programs are now on cable channels and I
was
trying to reduce my monthly bills so decided to have things in an
order
of preference.
So fortunately, one night I was scanning through all these
channels
to find something interesting, I got this station and the topic
that host
was talking about was so interesting I decided to listen more.
Later I
found out it was 680 The Fan sports radio in my beautiful city,
and it
was Jason Smith on air (All *Night with Jason Smith* on ESPN
Radio). From that moment that program became my new gig;
and as
part of his show, he had a segment called "Way or No Way" and
always
had weird stories or statement, many times not all about sports.
I think
he is intelligent and funny.
He would ask the caller to answer if his statement, news, or story
is "way," which means true, or "no way," that indicates it's not
true.

Something similar happened that made me think of that "Way and No

Way" segment. Elton John, a celebrity singer, played and entertained at

Rush Limbaugh's wedding for a million dollars. As we all know, Rush

Limbaugh is a conservative and hosts a popular conservative

talk radio show. Elton John is not a conservative; and in most

people's minds, that would have been a "no way" situation. But it was

"Equal rights and justice for all people"

105

a true story, so it was "way" because Elton John agreed on the

invitation to perform. That was his business and had nothing to

do as per

their opposite political ideologies and disagreement on issues.

So as common people, we should not be fooled and allow some

of

our political leaders or influential people in our societies turn us

into

political extremists or foot soldiers basically for their selfish

political

ambitions, with the intention of implementing some of their

political

agendas or impose some of their radical ideologies, which in

most cases

not of benefit to the masses but only themselves and their peers.

"Equal rights and justice for all people"

106

The Red Phone Controversy

he significance of the red phone or the red telephone in politics
especially in international politics. This phone, according to
wikipedia.com, is the hotline that allowed direct
communication
between the leaders of Russia and the United States and linked
the White House via the National Military Command Center
with the
official residence of the president of Russia during the Cold War.
After the Cold War, the red phone remained as the hotline to
reach
the president in case of national emergency and other important
issues
that the president must be notified immediately for his or her
approval
or consent. In the recent presidential election, in one of the
developed
world, the red phone controversy was started by a woman
presidential candidate in that race to make a point about how
women are
more capable to answer the red phone at the dawn of the night,
because
they are used to waking up to nurse their infants at that time of
the day. It
was a very good analogy because as men, 95 percent of us will
prefer to
sleep and will find it so inconvenient to wake up at that hour of
the night
to take care of our infants, especially when the mother is
available,
I could not comprehend how the red phone issue was blown out

of proportion and was actually one of the controversies to disqualify

the woman presidential candidate in that race. That kind of controversy

was never brought up before in all the previous elections because all

the presidential candidates were all men. I agreed it was a woman

presidential candidate started that red phone controversy, but some of the

other presidential candidates and their campaign managers blew it out

of proportion and started the uproar about the incompetence of women

"Equal rights and justice for all people"

T

107

as a president. Seeing women in that role was bothersome to
most men.

Initially when the red phone controversy was brought up, I thought
it was a joke until it was actually getting some quality airtime that could
have been used to address the masses on substantial issues of benefit
and their plans on how to achieve their goals.

So, it is logical to argue that women are more qualified
than men for this kind of responsibility. Psychologically women have
the natural ability to endure; they can manage pain and suffering
better. Sometimes as a man, I could not comprehend the discomfort and
pain they go through especially during pregnancy, between eight to ten
months. Sometimes I imagine what women go through during pregnancy.

For instance, most days when I leave for work, I have to carry my laptop
in a backpack, some books, my lunch bag, and my briefcase.
I used to live in a high-rise building. My unit was almost halfway
up in a thirty-four-level high-rise. I loved it up there because of the
scenery of my beautiful city especially at night. Sometimes it was as if
I was in a dream land, *but* I have to carry the load every day from my
unit all the way to the parking deck. That was kind of strenuous, but I

consoled myself, imagined that as a good exercise. And also during the

trip to my car, sometimes I meet nice people to have a quick but friendly

chitchat. Sometimes, those kinds of brief encounters helped to start my

day—positive energy.

Could you imagine what women go through to carry that precious

baby for that long before given birth? Then start nursing him or her, some

sleepless nights. So, answering the red phone should *not* be a problem.

Some of my friends argued that men helped with the night duty too,

nursing their baby; but to be sincere, you cannot compare the percentage

of men that offer this great service to help for the existence of human

beings. Most of us men will help with that once in a blue moon. So

this is also one of the many reasons a woman is better qualified to be a

president.

Sometimes, I wish we could stop applying this double standard, to be

more sensitive to women's advancement in life. Many times, we pretend

as if we care so much about them, especially in most of the developed

countries as part of showing respect to women. Men say, "Ladies first."

And if we really meant that and not just being sarcastic, then that should

"Equal rights and justice for all people"

108

be one of the many reasons why we should consider electing women

as presidents. *Ladies first* must apply to women being in the

position of power as a president too and should not only be just a norm

for exhibiting social etiquette, but applying this in our political system

too.

"Equal rights and justice for all people"

109

Women Are Compassionate, which equals Ability to Lead

I

s it really a man's world? Because sometimes I wonder how and why
    some of our leaders get away with fornication, adultery and indecent
    acts in general. It's amazing, and I could not comprehend seeing most
    of their wives forgiving them and sometimes coming on TV to show some
    solidarity. As men, most of us have skeletons in our cupboards; and if it's
    one of the criteria not to be qualified to be a president, I bet most men will
    never be. I live in a developed country. Unfortunately, my most favorite
    president was in trouble for a while during his presidency, accused of
    this kind of issue, and his opponents were bent on impeaching him.
    It was really a sad moment for me. I did not want to believe what
    he was just accused of. It's natural to want to side with people you care
    about. For instance, tell any parent their son just stole a cat. I bet they will
    be in denial, and like I use to argue then, "innocent until proven guilty."
    But deep down I was so irritated and hoped it could all be resolved; then

we could all forgive and forget. Some of us forgave him but
still talk about it from time to time; but some, especially his
opponents,

never forgive and forget. I like him personally, not necessarily
based

on his political achievements, although he tried his best for the
masses.

Some people argued he was at the right place at the right time
and did

not really do much. Don't we all wish to be at the right place at
the right

time?

I do appreciate the judicial system in most of the developed
world

and also, the freedom of speech because I am originally from a
Third

"Equal rights and justice for all people"

110

World country. Leaders committing such indecent acts are normally

categorized as macho men, and even when you are against their way, of

life, you better not speak out about it or else you will end up disappearing

from the face of this earth. That's how powerful and oppressive these

leaders are in the Third World countries. As men we assume we have all

the great qualities and will to lead; but come to think of it, those in glass

houses should not throw stones.

"Equal rights and justice for all people"

111

Past and Present World Leaders' Quotes

P

eople's leaders are true leaders, and they are generally compassionate, selfless, and always do their best to improve the life of the common
people (the masses). They lead, although they are never flawless
and sometimes could be rigid about some of their political beliefs and
ideologies. But overall, they try as much as possible to make things better
for the masses. The true leaders can never be compared at any level to the
one faking to be a leader because the latter is in politics mainly for *his*
own political gains, for *his* families and associates. I use the phrase "for
his" because men are dominating the countries' presidential positions
from time immemorial and hopefully with more awareness, we could all
support all these *overqualified* women political leaders and grant them
the equal opportunities finally to start leading us.

Great leaders talk with wisdom, and sometimes we take some of
their phrases out of some of their speeches as quotations. Most of them
are visionaries, skilled, and affectionate. All these are great qualities to

lead, and as for a woman president, her additional quality will be her

natural nurturing ability, compassion, and patience.

"Patience is the companion of wisdom.'

—Saint Augustine (354-430)

"Equal rights and justice for all people"

112

"Ask not for what your country can do for you; ask for what you can do

for your country".

—John F. Kennedy (1917-1963)

"Americans . . . still believe in an America where anything's possible.
They just don't think their leaders do".

—Barack Obama

"I leave you, hoping that the lamp of liberty will burn in your bosoms

until there shall no longer be a doubt that all men are created free and

equal".

—Abraham Lincoln (1809-1865)

"I dream of the realization of the unity of Africa, whereby its leaders

combine in their efforts to solve the problems of this continent. I dream

of our vast deserts, of our forests, of all our great wilderness".

—Nelson Mandela

"Leaders are made, they are not born. They are made by hard effort,

which is the price which all of us must pay to achieve any goal that is

worthwhile".

—Vince Lombardi

"A nation which has forgotten the quality of courage which in the past has

been brought to public life is not as likely to insist upon or regard that

quality in its chosen leaders today—and in fact we have forgotten".

—*John* F. Kennedy

"We can't allow the world's worst leaders to blackmail, threaten, hold

freedom-loving nations hostage with the world's worst weapons".
—*George* W. Bush

"Men make history and not the other way around. In periods where there

is no leadership, society stands still. Progress occurs when courageous,

skillful leaders seize the opportunity to change things for the better".
—*Harry* S. Truman

"Equal rights and justice for all people"

113

"Imagination is more important than knowledge. Knowledge is limited.

Imagination encircles the world".

—*Albert* Einstein (1879-1955)

"The whole life, from the moment you are born to the moment you die, is

a process of learning".

—*Jiddu* Krishnamurti (1895-1986)

"The mystic bond of brotherhood makes all men one".

—*Thomas* Carlyle (1795-1881)

"Surround yourself with only people who are going to lift you higher".

—*Oprah* Winfrey (1954-)

"Freedom is the last, best hope of earth".

—*Abraham* Lincoln (1809-1865)

"Leaders must be close enough to relate to others, but far enough ahead

to motivate them".

—*John* C. Maxwell

"Follow your instincts. That's where true wisdom manifests itself".

—*Oprah* Winfrey (1954-)

"The great leaders have always stage-managed their effects".

—*Charles* de Gaulle

"Great leaders are almost always great simplifiers, who can cut

through argument, debate and doubt, to offer a solution everybody can

understand".

—*Colin* Powell

"A luta continua, victoria e certa means *"The struggle continues, victory*

is certain".

—*Anonymous* leader

(Source: BrainyQuotes.com)
"Equal rights and justice for all people"

114

Quotes from Others

"If you are not for us, you are against us".

    —Unknown leader

    "Common people, you are never patient, leadership is not easy as you

    think, and I promise to take care of your problems if you elect me again".

    —Unknown leader

    "I am your home-boy, so you are obliged to elect me as your president".

    —Unknown leader

    "Equal rights and justice for all people"

115

Political Quiz

Here's a quiz to determine if you are a political extremist or moderate.

Once you finish answering these questions, you can determine if you are

either an extremist, moderate, liberal or conservative.
Yes
1. Elton John played and entertained at the
Rush Limbaugh wedding, and you are really
disappointed.
2. President Obama is not a United States of
America citizen.
3. President Bush lied about the weapons of
mass destruction (WMD) in Iraq because of
the failed oil deal for the Bush family.
4. Republicans sabotaged the oil well in the Gulf
of Mexico so they can win the US presidential
election in 2012.
5. All illegal immigrants, especially Mexicans,
should be deported to Arizona State, USA.
6. President Obama caused the recession.
7. President Obama should give everybody
legally in the United States of America one
thousand dollars credit every month.
8. President Obama should take money from all
the rich people and distribute it to the poor
folks.
"

Maybe No

116

Yes

9. All black people do not like white people.

10. All white people do not like black people.

11. Oprah Winfrey said she will be the first woman president in the United States of America in 2016.

12. President Bush caused the financial meltdown on purpose to bring down the United States of America.

13. Everybody must carry a gun.

14. President Obama is a socialist sponsored by a worldwide socialist group.

15. Women are *not* qualified to be presidents especially in the developed countries.

Maybe No

"Equal rights and justice for all people"

117

Coexisting

Attention!

To everybody in the world, our agenda *must be equal opportunity for*

all, no matter your race, ethnicity, religion, or gender. We can all
(Design based on Piotr Mlodozeniec's coexist Seam design entered in an art

contest hosted by the Museum of the, Israel)

"Equal rights and justice for all people"

COEXIST

118

Your response to the
political quiz and your group

Ö If you answered *"yes" to more than three questions, you are
an extremist.* You could be either a right-wing extremist or a
left—wing extremist.

Ö You are a *moderate if you answered "maybe" to three or more
questions.*

Now you can read the breakdown or the interpretation for each
question.

1. What's wrong if Elton John entertained at Rush Limbaugh's
wedding? They have different political ideologies
and stands on issues *but* that should not make them enemies.
Elton John is an entertainer doing his job, and Rush Limbaugh
has the money to pay him for his service. I heard some House
representatives and senators from different political parties
used to socialize, and that some were even close friends. But
unfortunately, nowadays most are restraining from that kind of
relationship because some people are becoming extreme with
their ideologies, so they see the other people that don't believe
in those ideologies as enemies. But politics is better for
the common people when our political leaders can give and take,
work together in harmony, and execute their agenda on time
instead of unnecessary long debates without any compromise, to
get results.

"Equal rights and justice for all people"

119

2. President Obama is a United States citizen, *period,* and we do not have to honor some people that are ignorant by explaining *what is not.*

3. President Bush did not lie about the weapons of mass destruction

(WMD). I am not playing a devil's advocate, *but* I do not believe President Bush intentionally lied about the WMD. It was just bad advice from the supposed experts. Also, if you're about to start a war and the leader of the *other* country continued to taunt you by saying, "That war will be the father of all wars," mere propaganda or whatever you want to call that kind of verbal attack would probably make you think your opponent is ready to *go all the way.* And in that scenario, the United States was in a better position as per war ammunitions. The United States assumed they were better, so that kind of verbal attack probably influenced their thinking that maybe Iraq was relying on another kind of weapon to win that war.

And if you still believe President Bush lied, just give that a second thought and imagine if it was true that Iraq had the WMD and used it. Everybody will rebuke whoever is in control of that developed nation at that moment. For instance, why did the United States not take a drastic action to destroy it and make the world a safe place? Also, imagine you had a dispute with somebody and went to his house, and he came out with his hands behind him posing as if he would attack you. You were already paranoid and assumed he was carrying a gun or a knife, even if your visit was to resolve your indifferences. It's natural, especially as men can be overly aggressive, to attack indiscriminately.

The Iraq war was just unfortunate, and actually there is nothing like a good war because there was no justification for

the death of thousands of innocent people, I don't mean just
the civilians but also the soldiers. I think if a woman was the
president, because of her patience and being more
compassionate
than men, that war could have been avoided. Somebody argued
that women are too emotional, but that might have led to a
better
decision, and that war might have been avoided, and a sanction
on Iraq instead. There is nothing like a good war; all wars are bad,

"Equal rights and justice for all people"

120

and the aftermath is always devastating. Hopefully the people of this world can make peace as much as possible; then we can all live in peace and harmony.

"Peace cannot be kept by force. It can only be achieved by understanding".

—Albert Einstein (1879-1955)

4. When you talk about patriotism, the United States now is on the top of that chart. They are proud of their colors (flag) and accommodating to all foreigners as long as they obey and respect the law of their land. That's why the United States is called the melting pot for all nations of the world. That's one of the many reasons why they call the United States *the land of opportunities* for all, no matter where you come from; and most of us wish our countries could elevate to this unique status. In addition to the opportunities, everybody that lives in the United States legally also have *freedom of speech,* although some individuals or group of people tend to abuse that. The incidence of 9-11 has affected a lot of things, so some laws were imposed to secure their motherland, which is fair. Also, the bad global economy has changed the way things were and encourage foreign influence to affect some necessities the people of the United States are accustomed to. *But* no citizen of this great nation will sabotage any of their infrastructures for political gains, so the Republicans did *not* sabotage the oil well in the Gulf of Mexico to win the presidential election in 2012.

5. Start programs and establish laws to make people that are already here legal and responsible residents. Nations spend too much money on deportation and imprisonment of illegal aliens (foreigners), but then, make your countries' borders less porous, to stop illegal immigration.

6. President Obama did *not* cause the recession, and this recession

was global.

7. The president of any nation could not just start printing money in

excess. That will result in inflation, as the economy experts put

it. So, President Obama giving everybody one thousand dollars

"Equal rights and justice for all people"

121

every month is not part of the solution to stop the recession. But to create *more jobs,* I suggest putting the deficit reduction at the back burner for now.

8. In a democratic system setup in any developed country, no president has the power to take money from all the rich people and distribute it to the poor. So, there is no way President Obama

can easily legislate that kind of proposal.

9. To say one race (white or black) hates all the people in the other race is just *pure* ignorance [This is the response to quiz items no. 9 and 10].

10. Oprah Winfrey *never* made that kind of statement, to be the first woman president in the United States, *but* we need

a woman president soon because they are more compassionate, patient, and have better ability to nurture. Then probably things would get better financially especially for the common people. Also, women can better promote peace and harmony in our world.

11. President Bush did *not* cause the financial meltdown in the United States because what caused the recession was a buildup of various mismanagement years back before he took over the office as president. One of the major mismanagements was that the government created avenues for the people to get credit to buy

their houses—the American dream. Especially people that were not qualified were approved too, and eventually people started defaulting on their loans, which led to the real estate bubble. Unfortunately, President Bush did not do much to correct things.

and he spent too much money on the wars he had inherited, and the war he started too. They started borrowing money from other countries, e.g., China, which resulted in a huge deficit, and other foreign influences that were negatively affecting the nation and her people because, as they say, "A beggar has no choice."

In another similar instance, most Third World countries had to drastically devalue their currency to meet the criteria to qualify for loans from the International Monetary Fund (IMF).

"Equal rights and justice for all people"

122

But unfortunately, most of that money was not spent for the purpose they (most of the Third World countries) got them for

to

start with. Most of the money from those loans was embezzled by their political leaders. Eventually these countries had to go back for more loans and continued to go more into debt. Apart from the devaluation of currency imposed on most of the underdeveloped countries (Third World), they were also

exposed

to foreign influences, which were directly or indirectly imposed on these countries. And most of those influences were negative, bad influences on the people in those societies, especially the common people (the masses).

It was so unfortunate to see those leaders embezzling all the money, and when asked, all of their response was always "Not me." That "not me" response from all those old folks reminded

me

of my nephews and nieces when they were under age ten. When you accused them about something, even before you completed your statement, their response was always "Not me." And as they grew older, whenever accused of some other things, most of

them

kept quiet as if your question was a rhetorical question. But if you pressed further, all you get was "Not me" over and over until you gave up. So the only conclusion was that maturity does not necessarily come with age, although most of us believe it's logical to say, "Maturity comes with age." And most of those political leaders and some people in general lack empathy.

Empathy is supposed to be one of the basic attributes of human beings (Homo *sapiens),* but I think some of us lack that basic attribute. Maybe with the advanced technologies and still evolving in this millennium, with the help of award-winning biologists and geneticists, maybe they will detect the gene that is missing that makes some human beings lack empathy, which is supposed to be one of the basic and unique attributes of all *Homo sapiens.* So, they would probably conclude that if some *Homo sapiens* lack that gene, then they will be grouped as "the missing link," or *Homo sapiens TML,* or just categorized as "TML"—no matter their race, gender, color, or country of origin. Then through that discovery, maybe most of our problems will be solved in this world of ours because most people, especially the common people, are suffering in the midst of abundant wealth.

"Equal rights and justice for all people"

123

12. Why should everybody carry a gun? Are we at war? If it's just a gun for recreational events (games), that's fine; but to arm yourself as if we are at war, is no fun. We'd rather live together in peace and harmony.

13. President Obama is *not* a socialist but a *democratically elected* president. Just because your ideology is different from others, it should not result in insulting others. Find a better way to promote

your ideologies instead of uncalled-for negative attacks.

14. Women are qualified and overdue to be democratically elected as presidents, especially in the developed countries.

"Woman will always be dependent until she holds a purse of her own".

—Elizabeth Cady Stanton (1815-1902)

"Equal rights and justice for all people"

Author's note

I

assumed you read this book already, and I connected with you one way or the other on this issue of appointing women as presidents, especially in the developed countries. By now you would have learned women can be very effective in the position of authority as presidents too. I am optimistic to see a woman president-elect in soon. Hope we continue to generate the awareness of the possibility. Whenever you plan, it's better to put a day to it; and most of the time, when you plan, you most likely accomplish that specific goal as scheduled or soon.

Equal *rights and justice for all people"*—Women are people too.

Sometimes, I wonder why women are still in bondage of modern slavery, and *it's about time* to start creating the awareness and honor women's rights and respect in our societies all over the world.

Believe in whatever you believe in, *but* love and respect yourself, also love and respect your neighbors. Do things for the betterment of humanity, and leave a good blueprint for the next generation to follow.

Do *not* be just a bystander in this journey of life. Be at peace with yourself and others. You will come to pass, like every other thing will come to pass too.

Lolu Adebayo
September 2024
124

References

Business Etiquette by Ann Marie Sabath

Do the Right Thing by Mike Huckabee

The End of Men by Eliza

The Audacity of Hope by Barack Obama

You Know I'm Right by Michelle Carusa-Cabrera

The Next Big Story by Soledad O'Brien with Rose Marie Arce

Aftershock: The Next Economy and America's Future by Robert B.

Reich

Conventional Idiocy: Why the New America Is Sick of the Old Politics

by Rick Sanchez

Article: Women in Politics by Jacqui K.

Aftershock: Protect Yourself and Profit in the Next Global Financial

Meltdown by David Wiedemer

125

126

Website Information Search

Please® Database, © 2007 Pearson Education, Inc - www.infoplease.com

Google Search – www.google.com

Online dictionary - www.yourdictionary.com

Online dictionary - en.wiktionary.org

Online book store – www.amazon.com

Great Quotes Source: www.todancewithangels.com/famousquotes

Free "encyclopedia" – www.wikipedia.org

Politics, Campaigns and Elections - www.uselections.com

Flags of countries - http://www.flagco.com/flags/worldflags

Fair Tax - www.fairtax.org

Public Radio – www.publicradio.org

"Equal rights and justice for all people"

127

Photo Credits:

Wikimedia Commons—http://commons.wikimedia.org

Source of all the photographs of Women World Leaders found in this

book, with the additional credits found below:

Joshua Sherurcij *(Photo of Mary McAleese)*

http://www.primeminister.govt.nz/ *(Photo of Helen Clark)*

Dirk Vordustraße *(Photo of Angela Merkel)*

Roger H. Goun *(Photo of Hillary Rodham Clinton)*

Agência Brasil, a public Brazilian news agency *(Photo of Ellen Johnson-Sirleaf)*

http://www.gpoaccess.gov/pictorial/index.html *(Photo of Nancy Pelosi)*

http://www.presidencia.gov.ar/ *(Photo of Cristina Fernandez de Kirchner)*

Roosewelt Pinhiero/ABR *(Photo of Tarja Kaarina Halonen)*

Margaret Thatcher Foundation. http://www.margaretthatcher.org/ *(Photo of Margaret Thatcher)*

"Equal rights and justice for all people"

DEDICATION

This book is dedicated to
My parents: Madam Ayodele Bernice
Adebayo, R.I.P. & Chief Elijah Ogidiolu
Adebayo, R.I.P.
My sisters: Clara, Veronica, Catherine,
Folashade
My brothers: Tim, Ola, Ade (R.I.P.), Tope,
Taiye
To Aisha Adebayo for her extraordinary
contribution and support and to everybody on
earth.
Let's promote love and peace so we can all live
in
harmony.
And finally, to all the women in the world, we
love
you!

****

Glossary

Cool: Used by the younger generation to indicate something of prestige

or in fashion

Dunk: To dip the ball into the cylinder of a basketball hoop

Fascists: A radical and authoritarian nationalist political ideology

Home state: My state of residence in the United States

Home team: Sports team in my state of residence in the United States

Home town: My country of origin

Holy books: Bible, Qur'an, Torah, Vedas, Tipitaka

Homo sapiens: Biological name for human beings

Mussolini: An Italian politician, he was one of the key figures in the

creation of fascism

My beautiful city: My state of residence in the United States

Pleasantries: Exchanging greetings when people meet

Stimulus: To use monetary or fiscal policy to stimulate the economy

129

Index

130

"Equal rights and justice for all people"

Roman Empire, 24

"Equal rights and justice for all people"

Walters, Barbara, 99
"Equal rights and justice for all people"

Don't miss out!

Visit the website below and you can sign up to receive emails whenever Lolu Adebayo publishes a new book. There's no charge and no obligation.

https://books2read.com/r/B-A-ZVMMC-ORBBF

Also by Lolu Adebayo

Why not a Woman President

About the Author

About the Author I am Lolu Adebayo, and I hold a bachelor's degree in biology and a master's degree in information technology. While I am not a politician or a political expert, my passion for advocating the important role women can play in politics has been with me since high school. I invite you to join me in raising awareness, fostering respect, and supporting women's contributions to our world. I have a love for reading non-fiction books with fun stories and interesting facts. I also enjoy children's literature, finding it both delightful and enlightening, like watching cartoon—often reminding me that there are lessons for adults within those pages. I believe that our world can become a better place when we respect one another, regardless of religion, sexual orientation, ethnicity, gender, or race. Empathy is essential for achieving peace, progress, and unity, and I hope to inspire others to embrace this vision.

About the Publisher

I am Lolu Adebayo, and I hold a bachelor's degree in biology and a master's degree in information technology. While I am not a politician or a political expert, my passion for advocating the important role women can play in politics has been with me since high school. I invite you to join me in raising awareness, fostering respect, and supporting women's contributions to our world. I have a love for reading non-fiction books with fun stories and interesting facts. I also enjoy children's literature, finding it both delightful and enlightening, like watching cartoon—often reminding me that there are lessons for adults within those pages. I believe that our world can become a better place when we respect one another, regardless of religion, sexual orientation, ethnicity, gender, or race. Empathy is essential for achieving peace, progress, and unity, and I hope to inspire others to embrace this vision.

www.ingramcontent.com/pod-product-compliance
Lightning Source LLC
Chambersburg PA
CBHW021143160726
47994CB00001B/61